Little Hands

WITHDRAWN

Create!

Art & Activities for Kids Ages 3 to 6

by Mary Doerfler Dall

Illustrations by Sarah Rakitin

Williamson Books W Nashville, Tennessee

Library of Congress Cataloging-in-Publication Data
Dall, Mary Doerfler.
    Little Hands create! : art & activities for kids ages 3 to 6 / Mary Dall ;
illustrations by Sarah Rakitin.
        p. cm. – (A Williamson Little Hands book)
    Includes index.
    ISBN 1-0-8249-8664-4 (pbk.)
        1. Handicraft--Juvenile literature. I Rakitin, Sarah, ill. II. Title. III. Series.

TT160.D25 2004
745.5--dc22   2004040872

Little Hands® series editor: Susan Williamson
Interior and cover design: Sarah Rakitin
Illustrations: Sarah Rakitin
Copy Editor: Vicky Congdon
Printing: Capital City Press

Williamson Books
An imprint of Ideals Publications
A division of Guideposts, Inc.
535 Metroplex Drive, Suite 250
Nashville, Tennessee 37211
800-586-2572

Manufactured in the United States of America
10 9 8 7 6 5 4 3 2 1

Kids Can!®, *Little Hands*®, *Quick Starts for Kids!*®, *Kaleidoscope Kids*®, and *Tales Alive!*® are registered trademarks of Ideals Publications, a division of Guideposts, Inc.

Little Hands Story Corner™, *Good Times*™, and *You Can Do It!*™ are trademarks of Ideals Publications, a division of Guideposts, Inc.

Notice: The information contained in this book is true, complete, and accurate to the best of our knowledge. All recommendations and suggestions are made without any guarantees on the part of the author or Ideals Publications. The author and publisher disclaim all liability incurred in conjunction with the use of this information and recommend strongly that adult supervision be given to all young children involved in art, crafts, and general activities at all times.

Dedication:

To all the preschool and kindergarten students I have known. They have truly been an inspiration. Their creativity and sense of wonder never cease to amaze.

Special thanks to Susan Williamson who "put it all together."

Special thanks, too, to my husband, Dan, who has learned to ask, "Are you saving this?" before throwing anything away . . .

Williamson Books grants permission to use selected art by Sarah Rakitin from her illustrations in *Awesome Ocean Science!* by Cindy A. Littlefield.

Permission to use Rubberball Productions' photograph of girl on cover is granted by Getty Images.

Contents

Odds 'n' Ends Art — 7

Pull-String Art — 8
Hole-Punch Magic — 10
Grocery Mesh-Bag Stitchery — 12
Popcorn People — 14
Foil Relief Art — 16
Masking-Tape Surprise — 18
Food-Color Fuzzies — 20
Coffee-Filter Flowers — 22
Potato "Snow" Scene — 26
Moovey-Groovy Art — 28
Stamping Sponge Fun — 31

3-D Sculpture — 33

Pretend Milk Glass — 34
Dryer-Lint Sculpture — 36
Egg-Carton Boat — 38
Grapevine Tree — 40
Robot Fun! — 42
Tissue Twists & Shapes — 44
Soap Sculpture — 46
Strip-Paper Sculpture — 48
String Things — 50
Straw Sculptures — 52

Critter Crafts — 54

Flitting Butterfly — 55
Terrific Turtles — 57
Stuffed Paper Animals — 59
Cotton-Ball Critters — 61

Snap-Lid Spiders — 63
Pinecone Reindeer — 65
Little Sea Creatures — 67
Octopus in a "Baggy" Aquarium — 69
Slippery Snakes — 71
Shredded Paper Bird's Nest — 73
Pencil-Shaving Sheep — 76

Creating Usable Art — 78

Marvelous Mesh Hat — 79
Carry-All Caddy — 81
Twisted-Paper Jewelry — 83
Wacky Hat — 86
Tube Hideaway — 88
Denim-Pocket Plaque — 90
Newspaper Mat — 92

Make-and-Play Art! — 95

Cork Town — 96
Magnet-Motor Mover — 98
Pocket Pop-Up Pal! — 100
Peanut Puppets — 103
Paper Pom-Poms — 105
Mixed-Up Picture Fun — 107
Tap, Tap, Tap Dancer — 109
Catch 'ems — 112
Special Day Crown — 114
Color-Your-World Viewer — 116

Index — 117

★ Self-Expression (and Fun!) Are Our Goals! ★

Children come to art, uninhibited, using all their senses. They bring vitality and a sense of wonder barely imaginable to the adult mind. By creating with their hands, hearts, and minds, children learn to express individuality, spontaneity, and imagination. They interpret the world around them through their art. They learn what will work and what won't. They see how things relate and fit together. The process is more important than the product.

As facilitators, we adults provide children with the opportunity and means to express themselves through art as well as offer encouragement and suggestions as they proceed. The outcome, however, should be unique to each child. While the adult may lead the project in a general direction, the child should bring his own interpretation to the process.

Art is not static. Happily, the days of identical projects created from a template, all lined up in a row, have been replaced by wildly different interpretations of an idea. While we are working toward an outcome using a particular process (e.g., making sponge prints), the resulting artistic expression of the child is unique. Creativity, self-expression, fun, and a sense of accomplishment are the true goals.

What's an age-appropriate activity? It is one that does not frustrate or embarrass a child. The degree-of-difficulty symbols really have nothing to do with age, nor with future intelligence or ability. They simply set a skill level needed to do a particular activity. Many times the activity seems simple enough, but it may involve fine motor skills that many preschoolers have not yet mastered. If a child is particularly interested in an activity, modify it to his skill level. And keep in mind that children develop these skills at very different rates.

Provide ample time, encouragement, and positive reinforcement for artistic expression. Help when a child asks, but let the child tell you what to do, rather than simply doing it for her. Then, let the child begin to work through any problems as she proceeds. This helps her apply problem-solving techniques and learn to resolve issues without conflict or frustration. Suggest that the child verbalize the steps of the process, for verbalization is another form of self-expression.

This book relies heavily on recycled items as art supplies. Environmentally, anything that encourages recycling is laudable. All too often we are quick to toss "junk" that could have a whole new life when given to a pair of little hands. The lowly egg carton has hundreds of artistic uses — many still waiting to be discovered! Reusing items is also cost-efficient, as it provides us with an almost unlimited supply of materials. As you begin to see potential in "trash treasures," little ones will invent more and even better ways to use these items.

The HELPING HANDS and MORE *LITTLE HANDS*® FUN! sections provide additional ideas and information for extending and enhancing the projects. If one is especially helpful or fun, make note of that suggestion for future reference. If you or the child come up with a new enhancement, record that, too. An activity book should "live and breathe" as a valuable, expandable resource that provides many years of use.

With that in mind, a section called *LITTLE HANDS STORY CORNER*™ accompanies some activities to provide additional stimuli by connecting the art activity to a story. Look for stories to accompany other crafts and encourage the child to discover other books related to the activities.

Parents and teachers are facilitators. We provide the opportunities, collect the necessary materials, and offer a nurturing, safe environment in which creativity can flourish. We supply, but little hands create!

Safety

In order to provide a safe environment for creativity, we must always keep child safety front and center. When working with young children, it is imperative that safety precautions are taken at all times. Most preschoolers are already safety-conscious in some respects, especially if they have a younger sibling and have been reminded by a parent or caregiver to "be careful" around the little one. But we want children to become fully involved in the projects, so it is the adult's responsibility to focus on safety.

▲ **Always work in a well-ventilated room,** especially when using permanent markers and glues or sprays.

▲ **Always use child safety scissors,** which are much improved over the ones we all used as children. Teach children how to walk with any scissors and how to hand them to another person.

▲ **Choking hazards.** Control the supply of small items that younger children may put in their mouths. Rather than putting small items on the table, let each child pick one or two out of your hands.

▲ **Sharp object warning.** Toothpicks can be very sharp and some types do not break readily. Be certain the children you are working with will not poke themselves or others with toothpicks and will not put them in their mouths.

▲ **Never leave young children alone near water.** Even an inch (cm) or two of water is a drowning hazard for small children. And never leave a small child in charge of a toddler near water.

▲ **Be certain that no child with a peanut allergy** is involved with or even in the same room with a project involving peanuts or peanut shells. Even if children do not eat the peanuts, some react simply by being around them. This is a very serious allergy and can be life-threatening. (The project on page 103 uses peanut shells.)

▲ **Never use a Styrofoam tray that held meat,** as it can carry salmonella even after being washed. Only reuse Styrofoam trays that contained fruits or vegetables and wash them first with soapy water.

✦ Odds 'n' Ends Art ✦

To the adults: Look around your house or school, and you will find many things that can be used to create works of art. Each item gives little hands a new tactile experience, whether it be feeling something fuzzy or items with rounded edges, like buttons. And each item stimulates new ideas for creating imaginative works of art, as children learn to improvise and use whatever is handy. Help children begin to look at the things considered "trash" and ask them how they might be used in a completely different way. Evaluate each item with an eye toward child safety, too. (Is it clean? Nonhazardous? Age-appropriate for a child to handle safely?) You will develop a sense of satisfaction when you realize that you're not only recycling, you're also opening a new world of possibilities to a child. So, start collecting and let the little ones start creating!

Pull-string Art

What will your picture look like
once you pull the string?
Something that is special
And very interesting!

Here's what you need:

Newspaper
Tempera paint
Lid from a plastic container
String, about 12" (30 cm)
Craft stick or twig
Sheet of light-colored paper

Here's what you do:

1. Cover your work surface with newspaper. Put some paint in the lid.

2. Dip the string into the paint, leaving about 1" (2.5 cm) unpainted at one end to hold. Use the craft stick or twig to push the string into the paint.

3. Fold the piece of paper in half, press it to make a crease, and then open it.

4. Place the painted string along the fold, using the craft stick or twig to help position it in the crease.

5. Refold the paper over the string.

6. Press lightly on the folded paper with one hand. With the other hand, pull the string up, down, and all around, then pull it out.

7. Open the paper and reveal your creation! Let it dry.

String art sure is nice!

▲ **Improvising with string.** How many ways can you think of to use a piece of string? Hmmm … one way might be to use string if your shoelace breaks. Can you name two ways? Three?

▲ **More string art.** Use several pieces of string, dipping each in a different color. Let each color dry before pulling a new color through your folded paper.

▲ **Hidden shapes.** Look for a shape in your picture. Outline it in crayon.

▲ **Make gift wrap and cards.** Make several pieces of PULL-STRING ART. Use as wrapping paper and tie a bow on the package with your pull string. Use them as greeting cards, too.

Helping Hands

✳ A painting smock or a big, old shirt may be in order for this activity.

✳ Give children complete freedom to do as they wish with this art. Some will be very precise and others will want the picture to be filled with color; there's no need to correct either approach.

✳ Introduce children to the idea of *improvising,* substituting what they have on hand for something they need.

Hole-Punch Magic

Where they will land you'll never know,
But making them is fun!
Your picture with these magic dots
Is a "one-and-only" one.

Here's what you need:

Newspaper
Hole punch
Colorful scrap paper
Old envelope (for storing your dots)
Paintbrush
White glue mixed with water (1 part glue
    to 1 part water) in a shallow bowl or
    plastic lid
Sheet of paper
Markers or crayons

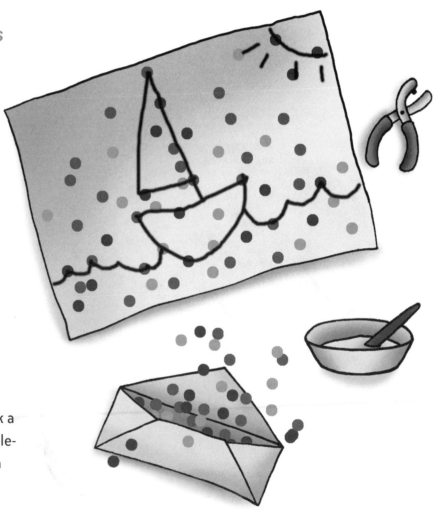

Here's what you do:

1. Cover your work surface with newspaper. Ask a grown-up helper to help you make a lot of hole-punch dots from the scrap paper. Shake them into the envelope and set them aside.

2. Using the paintbrush, spread the glue-water mixture on about a quarter of the sheet of paper. Sprinkle some hole-punch dots onto the wet glue. Repeat for the other quarters of the paper.

3. When the picture is dry, look for hidden shapes and pictures formed by the dots. Use the markers or crayons to connect the dots, or outline the shapes you see.

What a colorful dotted design!

Helping Hands

✳ If children have difficulty picking up small dots, tear up larger pieces of paper for this activity.

✳ For older children, set out bowls of paper dots and shapes, as well as seeds, so that they can purposefully design their pictures. Put unthinned glue in a lid and provide cotton swabs for applicators.

✳ Ask children to describe what they see when they look at their pictures.

More Little Hands® fun!

▲ **Colorful dots.** Separate the dots by colors in several bowls. Can you sprinkle only the red dots on your picture? The yellow ones? Your favorite color? How about sprinkling white, fluorescent, and yellow dots onto dark-colored paper?

▲ **Mix it up.** Drop bits of yarn, string, and seeds on the glued surface. Use decorative punches (they punch out different paper shapes); mix the shapes with the dots. Mix glitter with the dots before you drop them onto the paper.

Grocery Mesh-Bag Stitchery

Don't throw away those mesh bags.
(They're great for art, you know.)
Go in and out of their big holes,
And you'll know how to sew!

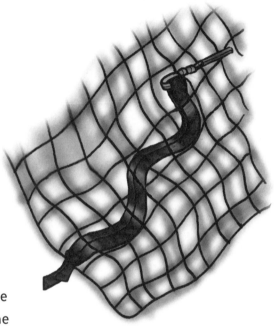

Here's what you need:

Twist tie
Yarn, string, ribbon, or colored cord
Scissors, for grown-up use
Mesh bag, like the ones oranges,
    onions, or potatoes come in

Here's what you do:

1. Ask a grown-up helper to make a sewing "needle" from the twist tie: Fold the twist tie into a U shape with one side a bit longer than the other. To make the hole, or "eye," through which to thread the yarn, twist the shorter side around the longer side.

2. Double-thread a piece of yarn, string, ribbon, or cord through the eye, pulling enough through to tie the double strand in a small knot.

3. Ask the grown-up helper to tie the end of the yarn or string to the mesh bag.

4. Use the needle to pull the yarn or cord in and out of the mesh bag's holes.

5. Take off the needle. Ask the grown-up to tie the other end to the bag.

What a nice bit of sewing you did!

More Little Hands® Fun!

▲ **Beads and buttons!** Add beads or buttons to the yarn or string as you pull it in and out of the mesh bag. Stretch your finished bag over a piece of cardboard and staple it in place.

▲ **Hang your bag.** Tie your mesh bag to a stick or tree branch. Tie ribbons or yarn to the edges of the bag and let them blow in the breeze.

▲ **For more fun with mesh bags,** see page 79.

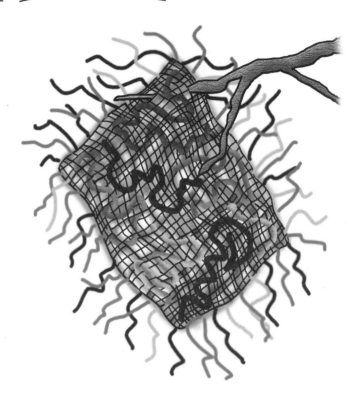

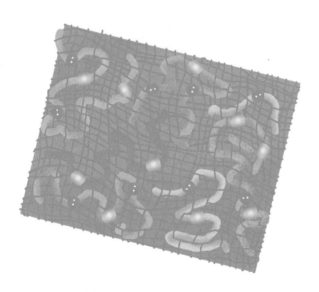

Little Hands Story Corner™

• *The Enormous Potato* by Aubrey Davis

Helping Hands

✻ This activity requires beginning fine motor skills. If children have any difficulty, move on to an activity that uses other skills. The timing of a child's fine motor skills development varies from one child to another.

✻ Some children may benefit from using plastic embroidery hoops when doing this activity. No need for the "sewing" to be in a straight line or to include each hole in the mesh bag.

Popcorn People

Popcorn, popcorn, everywhere —
Let's use it for some art!
Make a face and add some hair,
Your person looks so smart!

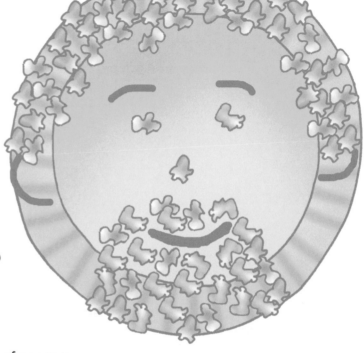

◢ Here's what you need:

Newspaper
Popcorn (popped) in a bowl
Paper plate (one per popcorn person)
White glue
Tempera paint and a paintbrush or
    markers (optional)

◢ Here's what you do:

1. Cover your work surface with newspaper. Set out the bowl of popcorn.

2. Use the paper plate for a face. Place some glue on the plate where you want the eyes to
    go. Then stick on the popcorn pieces. Continue gluing and adding popcorn pieces
    to make the nose, mouth, and ears.

3. Make popcorn hair, eyebrows, a beard or mustache, or whatever you wish.
    Let the glue dry. Use paint or markers to color the popcorn, if you like.

4. Now wash your hands and enjoy a popcorn snack!

Your popcorn people look great!

Tim

More Little Hands® fun!

▲ **Make a hat and some earrings.** Make and decorate a special paper hat for your popcorn person. Glue some popcorn on the ears for earrings or on the hat for a pom-pom.

▲ **Colorful popcorn!** Place some popcorn in a bag with dry paint powder to color it. Make a colorful popcorn person or a picture with it.

Helping Hands

✳ Help children visualize a person's face. Discuss the order of the eyes, nose, and mouth from the top of the head to the bottom. Let each child look in an unbreakable mirror to see how features are placed on a face.

✳ Popcorn is wonderful for making images of clouds, snow (or falling snowflakes), cottontails on bunnies, and tree blossoms, and for adding another dimension to any drawings that children make.

✳ Popcorn is large enough to help younger children begin making the transition from gross motor skills to fine motor skills as they work with it.

Foil Relief Art

It's fun to make these pictures,
Because they seem more real.
They are a special kind of art —
A kind that you can feel!

Here's what you need:

Newspaper
Pencil
Small piece of cereal-box cardboard
White glue
Aluminum foil
Black crayon (optional)

Here's what you do:

1. Cover your work surface with newspaper. With your pencil, draw a simple picture directly onto the cardboard. The bigger the shapes, the better.

2. Using the white glue like a pen, draw over your picture with a thick bead of glue. Let the glue dry completely.

3. When it's dry, cover the cardboard with the foil.

4. Rub your fingers gently along the foil so it fits tightly over and around the "glue bumps." Press along the sides of the bumps, as you want them to show.

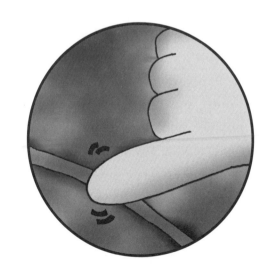

5. If you like, rub the black crayon over the cracks and folds to make the design show up even more, but be careful not to tear the foil.

can you see your relief art?

can you feel your relief art?

More Little Hands® fun!

▲ **Play with a "magic bag."** Fill a small paper bag with easily identifiable items that have different textures and shapes. Reach in and touch one item. Tell what it feels like. Can you guess what it is without looking?

▲ **Hang it up!** Mount your design on a piece of burlap or other material and hang it in your room. Or, make holes on each end at the top, loop yarn through the holes, tie, and hang.

▲ **Big and bold!** Put pieces of string on the white glue before it dries. Now when you add the foil, the design will stand out more boldly. Or, glue small, fairly flat items to the cardboard design before putting on the foil. Try using pieces of dry spaghetti, yarn, or some flat buttons.

Helping Hands

✳ This project helps children use their sense of touch in creating and identifying objects and shapes.

✳ Keep the drawings and designs very simple. Your example should be a single shape.

Masking-Tape Surprise

What is hiding under there?
What magic will escape?
When your picture is all dry,
Just pull away the tape!

▨ Here's what you need:

Newspaper
Masking tape (see HELPING HANDS, page 19)
Paper
Tempera paint and paintbrush, markers,
  or crayons

▨ Here's what you do:

1. Cover your work surface with newspaper. Place the masking tape any way you choose on your paper.

2. Paint or color the whole page, going right over the tape.

3. When the paper is dry, carefully peel away the tape.

What surprise do you see on your paper?

More Little Hands® fun!

▲ **Surprise! How'd that happen?** Can you tell how you made that tape design? What did the masking tape do?

▲ **Tape a letter.** On a new piece of paper, put the tape down in the shape of a big letter. Maybe you'll want to make the first letter of your name. Now follow the directions again. What surprise do you have when you remove the tape?

▲ **Add more colors.** Put more tape on the paper in different areas and paint or color again, this time with different colors. Remove the tape. Are you surprised by what you see?

Helping Hands

✳ To prevent the tape from tearing the paper when it's removed, have children tape it to their clothes first so that it isn't as sticky. Then place it on the paper.

✳ If a child makes the first letter of her name, ask her to draw things around her letter that start with the same letter sound.

Food-Color Fuzzies

fuzzy, wuzzy caterpillars?
A big, bright fuzzy bug?
What are those furry critters
crawling on your paper rug?

▨ Here's what you need:

Newspaper

Water

Sheet of art paper, light-colored construction
     paper, or inexpensive watercolor paper

Food coloring

Fine-tipped markers, in dark colors

Child-safety scissors

▨ Here's what you do:

1. Cover your work surface with newspaper. Wet the
piece of paper; shake off the extra water.

2. Sprinkle a few drops of food coloring on the paper in
different places.

3. Let the color drip and run, tilting the paper a bit to
keep the colors moving.

4. Let the paper dry.

5. Look at the fuzzy shapes. Do you see any little critter
shapes? Use markers to add wings, pincers, legs,
heads, tails, or whatever you wish, or just outline the
shapes you see.

6. Fringe the paper edges and decorate it like a rug.

My, what beautiful crawling creatures you have created!

▲ **Can you see them?** Tear a sheet of green paper and a sheet of bright red or orange paper into bits and pieces. Put them in a container. Step outside onto some green grass and toss the bits of paper in the air. Then see how many pieces of paper you can pick up in two minutes.

Sort the picked-up paper by color. Count each pile. How many of each? Was it harder or easier to find the green pieces? If you said harder, then you now know why it is sometimes very hard to see bugs on rugs or trees. They are *camouflaged,* or colored so that they blend in with their surroundings. Very clever, don't you think?

▲ **Three-dimensional art!** Cut out the fuzzies. Glue them to one end of a little accordion-folded piece of paper (see HOW TO MAKE ACCORDION FOLDS, page 23) and glue the other end of the folded paper to your "rug." You just made your fuzzies 3-D!

Coffee-Filter Flowers

Flowers are so pretty that
Sometimes it's hard to choose
The color you like best —
So, make a lot of hues.

Here's what you need:

Newspaper
Coffee filters or sheets of 8 ¹/₂" x 11" (21 x 27.5 cm)
    lightweight paper
Watercolor paints
Paintbrush
White glue
Drinking straws

Here's what you do:

1. Cover your work surface with newspaper. Place the coffee filters or paper on the newspaper.

2. Decorate the filters or papers using the watercolors. Let dry.

3. If you are using sheets of paper, accordion-fold your painted papers (see How to Make Accordion Folds, page 23). Keep it folded tightly.

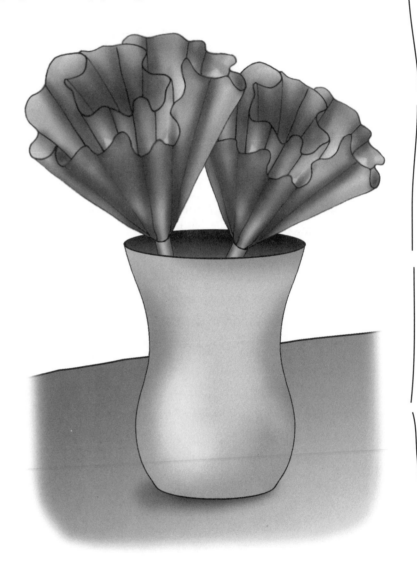

4. Gather the filters at the bottom and twist. Or, fold the paper in half, lengthwise.

5. Put some glue on the twisted bottom or the folded middle. Insert the glued piece into the opening of a drinking straw. You may have to "squash" the bottom a bit for it to fit. Ask a grown-up for help, if you like.

6. Now, fan open your paper flowers, pulling them gently apart at the tops. Display them in a vase. (See vases to make on pages 25 and 34.)

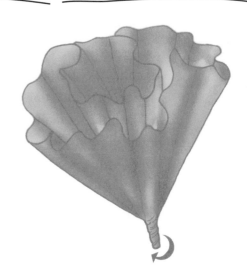

Are your flowers just starting to bloom or are their petals wide open?

How to Make Accordion Folds

1. Starting at the right edge of your paper, fold a flap to the left.

2. Then, turn your paper over and fold another flap to the left.

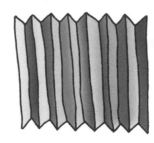

3. Repeat until your paper looks like an accordion.

▲ More flower art! Cut a coffee filter or colored paper into leaf shapes and tape them to the straw "stem." Use cupcake liners to make some smaller paper flowers to go in your bouquet. Add dots of white glue to your flowers. When dry, they will look like dewdrops.

▲ How many colors? Flowers come in so many colors and shapes. Look in a flower garden or flower shop. How many dark colors do you see? How many light colors? Do you see any black flowers? If you said no, you're right. There aren't any black flowers, but some of the dark purple flowers, like some tulips, look almost black.

Helping Hands

✳ The coffee filters' texture allows the watercolors to be absorbed and to spread for a nice effect. Some children may prefer to color sheets of paper instead, so they have bolder colors and more control over where the color goes.

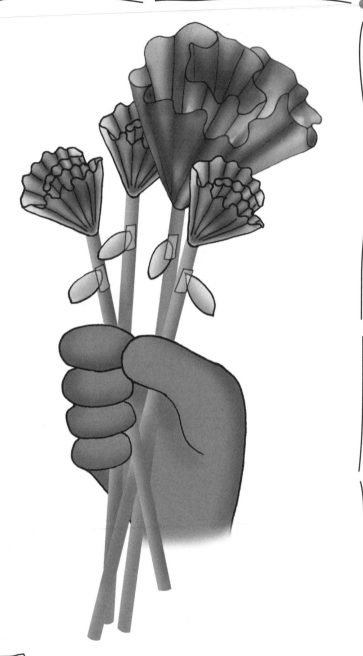

▲ **Plant some seeds.** If you have a sunny window, you can grow flowers from seeds. Fill an 8-ounce (250-ml) paper cup with potting soil. Poke four flower seeds (nasturtiums, marigolds, and zinnias are easy to grow) about $1/4$" (5 mm) into the soil and cover lightly with more soil. Water until wet but not soaking. Place on the windowsill (in a shallow dish or on a protective coaster) and water enough to keep the soil moist but not soggy. Now watch your flowers grow!

▲ **Make a vase.** Decorate a soup can, a jar, or a paper cup to hold your flowers. You can wrap it in construction paper, glue twine around it, or decorate it with small pieces of torn paper to make a mosaic. Now, when you help set the table for dinner, put your vase with the flowers in the middle for a centerpiece.

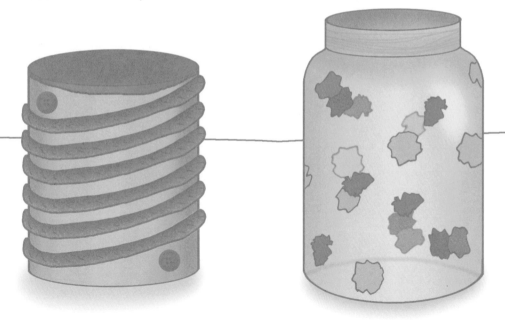

Potato "Snow" Scene

If you eat potatoes,
You may already know.
Instant mashed potatoes
Look a lot like snow!

Here's what you need:

Newspaper

Pencils

Sheet of dark-colored construction paper

Crayons or markers

White glue mixed with water (1 part glue
  to 1 part water) in a shallow bowl or
  plastic lid

Paintbrush

Instant mashed potatoes

Here's what you do:

1. Protect your work surface with newspaper. Draw trees, mountains, a house, or any snowy scene you'd like on your paper. Color them in.

2. Brush the glue/water mixture on the paper where you want to see fluffy "potato snow."

3. Sprinkle instant potatoes onto the glued areas. Press very lightly. Shake off the excess. Let dry.

4. Add more snow to the treetops or rooftops, if you like, using some glue without water.

Do you live where it snows a lot, just sometimes, or never at all?

More Little Hands® fun!

▲ **Let it snow!** No matter where you live, you can make your picture look even colder and snowier. Add glitter to the potato flakes. Use white glue directly from the bottle to add icicles to your snow scene (they will dry almost clear). Brrr!

▲ **Talk about snow!** Tell someone who has never seen real snow what snow feels like, tastes like, and looks like. What noise does it make under your boots? Then share your favorite snow-day moments! Never seen snow? Then tell someone what it's like to live where it's warm all year long.

Little Hands Story Corner™

• *The Snowy Day* by Ezra Jack Keats
• *Snow Music* by Lynne Rae Perkins

Moovey-Groovy Art

Make a collage with moving parts?
Wow! That's in the groove.
Art is never quite the same
When what you make can move!

✐ Here's what you need:

Plastic packaging shapes from store-bought items
Newspaper
Heavy paper or cereal-box cardboard
White glue
Decorations: small brightly colored beads, uncooked
  pasta, unpopped popcorn, buttons, jingle bells, etc.

✐ Here's what you do:

1. Collect a variety of small clear plastic packaging shapes like the ones covering scissors, hairbrushes, and small toys. (These are usually in the same shape as the item they are covering in the package.)

2. Cover your work surface with newspaper. Set out the shapes.

3. Pick up each shape and look at it, gently rubbing your hand over and around it. When you find several shapes you like, arrange them on the paper or cardboard.

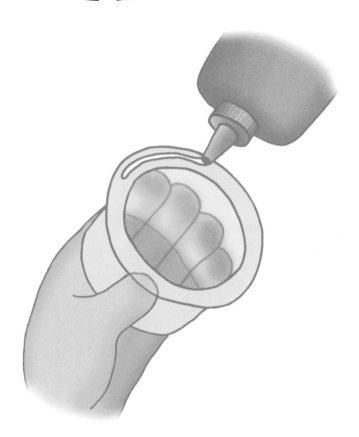

4. Lift each shape, one at a time, and carefully put glue all around the bottom edge.

5. As you put the shape in place on the paper, slip the decorative items under it, being careful not to move the shape around.

6. Hold the glued shape in place until it dries.

7. Shake your art and the inside decorations will move around.

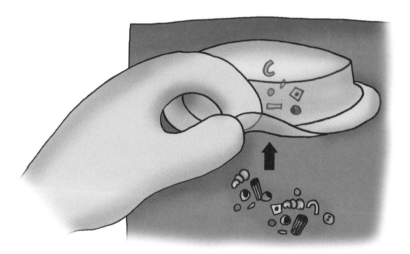

Isn't that cool? Does your art move and make a noise, too?

More Little Hands® fun!

▲ **Is that art?** Do you think something that moves is art? When someone says, "Let's make art today," what do you think you are going to be doing?

▲ **How many senses?** Your five senses are seeing, hearing, tasting, touching, and smelling. How many senses did you use in your MOOVEY-GROOVY ART?

Helping Hands

✳ Help children realize that they have an entire "tool package" with them all the time — their five senses. Name several things that children do every day (answer the phone, turn off a light) and let them name the sense they are using. This is a good opportunity to introduce sight- and hearing-challenged people and to discuss how they *compensate* by using other senses.

Little Hands Story Corner™

• *Fun With My 5 Senses* by Sarah A. Williamson

Stamping Sponge Fun

Make sponges used for stamping
In many shapes and sizes.
Then design your very own papers
To wrap up some surprises!

Here's what you need:

Newspaper
Plain white tissue paper or construction paper
Precut sponges (or make your own, see MORE
    LITTLE HANDS® FUN!, page 32)
Paint in a shallow lid or dish
Odds and ends like corks, buttons, etc.

Here's what you do:

1. Cover your work surface with newspaper.

2. Spread out the paper you are going to use to make your
own wrapping paper.

3. Dip each sponge in the paint and apply the stamps to
the paper in a haphazard way or in a pattern. Use the
odds and ends as stamps, too.

Your sponge art is so nice, let's hang it on the wall!

▲ **Make your own sponge shapes.** It's easy and fun, especially when you use dehydrated sponges (available at craft shops). They are super thin, so it's easy to trace any shape on them and cut it out with grown-up help. Then put a few drops of water on the sponge shape. Like magic, it will grow into a normal-sized sponge. (Be sure your hands are perfectly dry when you work with these sponges because *any* moisture causes them to grow.)

▲ **Stamp sea, land, and sky animals!** In your mind, divide a large sheet of paper into the sea, the land, and the sky. Using animal-shaped sponges, stamp sea animals at the bottom of the paper, land animals in the middle, and flying animals at the top.

▲ **Create new colors!** Try stamping a blue paint animal and then immediately stamping the same animal in yellow on top. See? You made a green animal! Red, yellow, and blue are called the *primary colors*, and we combine them to make all the other colors we know. See if you can create purple or orange from these primary colors.

Little Hands Story Corner™

• *Sea, Sand, Me* by Patricia Hubbell

• *Sea Life Art & Activities* by Judy Press

Helping Hands

✳ This activity is a great way to introduce sponges and talk about how natural sponges are animals from the sea, while synthetic sponges are made in factories. Allow children to examine natural and man-made sponges and talk about the different uses for them.

★ 3-D Sculpture ★

Children love almost anything that is three-dimensional: They love to hold things in their hands, to play with objects, and to walk around a sculpture, viewing it from every angle. And, of course, they love to build structures. Simple household items such as shoe boxes, plastic juice containers, straws, pieces of scrap wood, and the like are catalysts for children to let their imaginations run free while constructing unusual shapes. Form and function change as children work with common items to produce uncommon results. Help children begin cutting, gluing, shaping, and building, as little hands and big imaginations create in three dimensions!

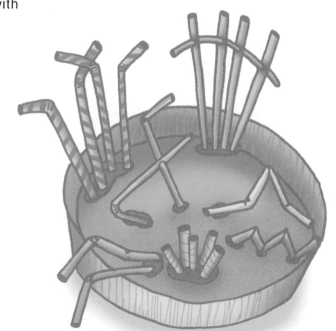

Pretend Milk Glass

This "milk glass" is a special glass —
It's white with small raised spots.
You can make a fancy vase
With lots and lots of dots.

Here's what you need:

Newspaper
White glue
Dried lentils
Clean juice can from concentrate, or other
    interesting container of your choice
Tempera paint, in white or pastel color
Paintbrush

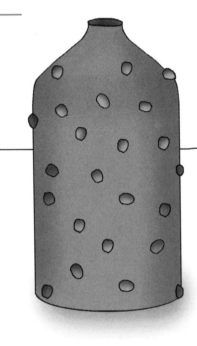
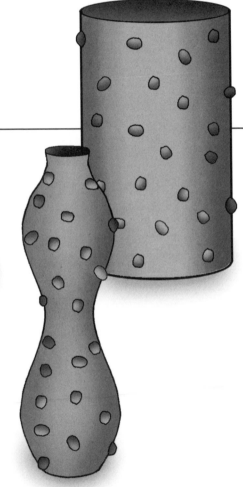

Here's what you do:

1. Cover your work surface with newspaper. Glue the lentils to the outside of the juice can or container.

2. When the glue is dry, paint the can, covering the lentils, too.

3. When dry, put on a second coat of paint.

Oh, you've made a lovely
holder for flowers or pencils!

More Little Hands® fun!

▲ **Add coffee-filter flowers** (see page 22) to the vase.

▲ **Use small shell or ABC pasta** instead of lentils.

Helping Hands

✳ This activity lends itself to a project for showing kindness and also for Mother's Day and other events. It is good practice for those working on fine motor skills, as the lentils are small enough to challenge those new to such fine work. You also might ask children to look around their grandparents' or older friends' homes for milk glass.

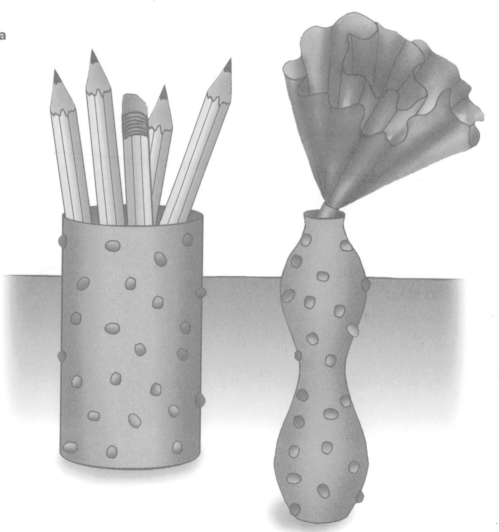

Dryer-Lint Sculpture

Just add a little water
So the lint becomes like clay.
Twist, mold, and squeeze it out.
Once dry, it'll stay that way.

Here's what you need:

Newspaper
Handful of dryer lint
Disposable aluminum pie plate or Styrofoam
    tray (from fruits or vegetables only)
Water
Tempera or poster paint
Paintbrush
Colored tissue paper, torn into scraps, or glitter

Here's what you do:

1. Cover your work surface with newspaper. Put the lint on the pie plate or tray.

2. Add water to the lint until it's quite wet, but not sopping.

3. Squeeze a lot of the water out as you begin molding the lint into a shape. Pour off the excess water.

4. Bend and twist the lint into anything you want — a crazy shape, a made-up monster, or whatever you'd like to create.

5. Place the pie plate or the tray in the sun and allow your lint sculpture to air dry.

6. Paint your creation. Before the paint dries, press on the paper scraps or sprinkle on some glitter.

Where will you place your sculpture?

More Little Hands® Fun!

▲ **It's sculpture.** Name three things that make your sculpture different from a picture that you draw.

▲ **Play a variation of Statues.** Take turns posing as a statue of someone doing something, such as a baseball player at bat (hold that swing!) or a person holding a baby. Walk around the statue (it's three-dimensional, of course!). What do you think the statue is doing?

Egg-Carton Boat

This sailing ship is lots of fun.
(It's not just any boat.)
What makes it extra-special is
The fact that it can float!

Here's what you need:

Newspaper
Empty Styrofoam egg carton
White glue, if needed
Scissors, only for adult use in cutting
　　egg-cup windows
Toothpicks
Paper to make flags, people, etc.
Fine-tipped permanent markers

Here's what you do:

1. Cover your work surface with newspaper. Close the egg carton, gluing it shut if necessary. Turn it upside down.

2. Ask an adult to carefully cut windows into the egg cups (top, middle, bottom). Fold the windows back on the sides like shutters. Or, cut circles like portholes.

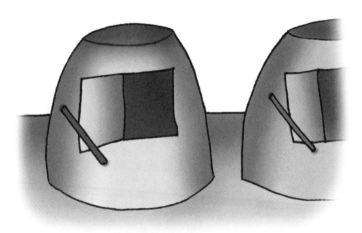

 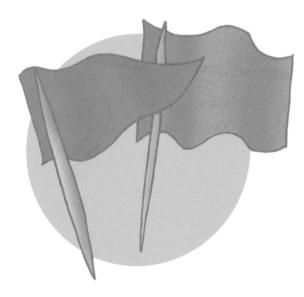

▲ **Have you ever been on a boat?** Tell your friends what you did when you went on a boat. Describe how it felt to be in the boat. Was the ride bumpy, smooth, or with gentle ripples?

▲ **Does it float?** Ask a grown-up to help you float your boat in the sink.

3. Slip toothpicks in at an angle to hold the windows open.

4. Make paper people for inside the boat and glue them to stand in the open windows. Make flags and glue them on toothpicks. Use them to decorate your boat.

Will you float your boat in the sink or in a basin?

Little Hands Story Corner™

• *The Sea House* by Deborah Turney Zagwyn

Grapevine Tree

First you get to eat some grapes,
Then use the stems for fun.
And oh, how nice it is to know
Each tree's a "one and only" one.

Here's what you need:

Newspaper
Bunch of grapes to eat (and share)
Small chunk of modeling clay
Styrofoam tray (from fruits or vegetables only)
    or disposable aluminum pie plate
Star stickers, buttons, or anything small you'd
    like to hang from the branches
Child-safety scissors
Thread
Paper, cotton balls, or cupcake liners

Note: No grapes? Small twigs from trees work
    fine, too.

Here's what you do:

1. Cover your work surface with newspaper. Eat the grapes!

2. Put the clay on the tray or pie plate and push the largest part of the grape stem into it.

3. Place the star stickers back to back on the branches. Or, cut lengths of thread and use them to hang buttons or other small items from the branches.

4. Cover the clay base with star stickers, a paper skirt, pulled-apart cotton balls, an inverted cupcake liner, or whatever decorations you like.

Your tree is wonderful — just like you!

More Little Hands® fun!

▲ **More tree art!** "Paint" the tree with white glue and sprinkle with glitter. Or, make a whole forest of trees. Want to design a whole village? Make buildings from cardboard milk cartons and then add lots of trees.

▲ **Tree-bark rubbings.** Find as many kinds of tree bark outdoors as you can. Hold paper against each tree trunk and rub a crayon over it. Now compare the different rubbings. Which ones are bumpy? Which ones are smooth?

Helping Hands

✳ If possible, take children for a walk and show them different kinds of tree trunks and tree bark. Have them touch each bark and use words like rough, smooth, bumpy, prickly, and raised to describe it.

✳ Show children pictures of different types of trees and discuss how the overall shapes differ.

⚙ Robot Fun!

Robots, robots, robots!
Made with things you've found.
Will yours go to Mars
or, never leave the ground?

◪ Here's what you need:

Newspaper
Child-safety scissors
Construction paper
Soda bottle, clean powdered-drink container,
    or shampoo bottle — with lids
White glue
Permanent markers
Egg carton or paper plate, yarn for hair, etc.
    (optional)

◪ Here's what you do:

1. Cover your work surface with newspaper. Cut a long strip
of colored paper that's about 1" (2.5 cm) wide.

2. Remove the lid from the container or bottle and place the
middle of the paper strip across the top. Put the lid back on
and seal it so that the paper "arms" stick out on both sides
as shown. (Add paper hands or claws to the ends, if you like.)

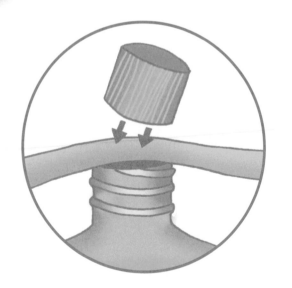

3. Fold a piece of paper in half and cut out a foot (or lots of feet!). Open the paper, and you will have two feet that are the same.

4. Glue the feet to the bottom of your robot/monster.

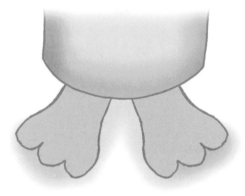

5. Decorate the lid as the face. If the lid is too small for a "face," glue a four-egg section of an egg carton or a paper plate to the top and decorate it. Or, turn the container or bottle upside down, making a huge head for your robot or monster.

▲ **More robot fun!** Glue gears from old watches, buttons, and beads to the body. Put unpopped popcorn, sand, bells, or dry rice in your container before you put the lid back on so that the robot makes noise when it walks.

▲ **Personal robots.** Would you like to have a robot of your own? What would you use it for?

Helping Hands

✳ Talk about robots and what they can do now. Show pictures of the robots that landed on Mars and ask children what they think robots will do in the future. Talk about what makes a robot different from a real person.

Tissue Twists & Shapes

Twist and turn the tissue
'Til it starts to curl and snake.
Create a silly structure.
What a great thing you can make!

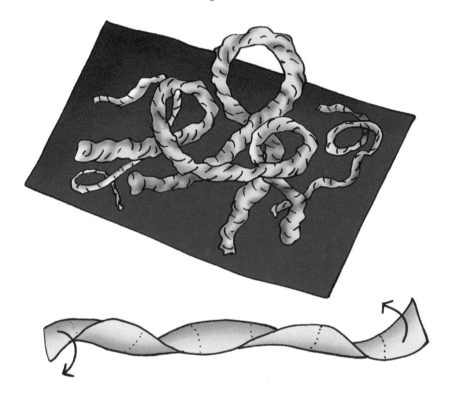

Here's what you need:

Newspaper

Strips of bathroom tissue and paper towel
(optional), about 3' to 4' (3 to 3.5 m) long

White glue

Heavy paper or cereal-box cardboard, in a
contrasting color to the tissue, if available

Markers or paint and paintbrush (optional)

Here's what you do:

1. Cover your work surface with newspaper. Holding each end of a strip of bathroom tissue, curl it in opposite directions. (You may want to work with a partner to help hold one end for you.) To make some thicker twists, use long strips of paper towels.

2. When the strip is curled and twisted, gently tie or knot it.

3. Glue the twisted shape onto the paper or cardboard.

4. Make more twists and add them to your sculpture.

5. Paint and decorate your sculpture.

Aren't you proud of your tissue-paper sculpture?

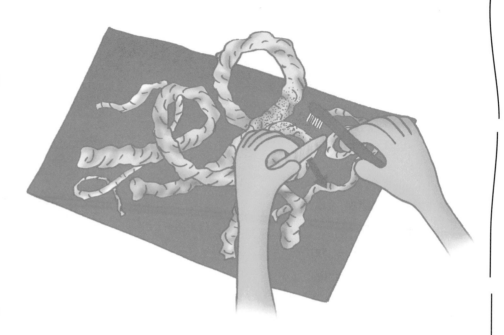

△ Sculpture extras. Use markers on your sculpture. Or, spatter paint on it. (Put paint on an old toothbrush. Hold it toward the sculpture. Pull a craft stick over the bristles toward yourself. The paint will spatter back away from you and onto the sculpture.) How about twists made from crepe paper streamers to go with your tissue twists?

△ Living sculpture. Standing up (or sitting in your chair), pretend that your feet are glued to one place on the floor. Stretch as far as you can in different directions without moving your feet. Gradually begin to twist your body, and then gently turn your body in different directions. Combine your stretch and your twist, and then hold that pose. If a digital camera is available, have someone take a picture of you, then look at it to see what kind of living sculpture you made.

More Little Hands® fun!

Helping Hands

✳ Using a digital camera when working and playing with children is a wonderful way to record special moments and to let a child see exactly what she has accomplished. Reviewing the varied forms of art that a child has made reinforces different types of art, too. Try to include the child in the photo with the piece of art. Then, let the child explain how she created the art.

Soap Sculpture

Soap's not just for washing —
Try some sculpting fun.
You'll have a cool soap sculpture
When _you_ decide it's done.

Here's what you need:

Newspaper
Bar of soap (unused)
Pencil or toothpick
Craft stick or butter knife for carving tool
Buttons, beads, or beans (optional)
Small box for stand (optional)

Here's what you do:

1. Cover your work surface with newspaper. Unwrap the bar of soap.

2. Using the pencil or toothpick, draw a big shape that fills most of the bar of soap.

3. Hold the bar firmly with one hand. With the other hand, use your carving tool to cut and shave pieces from it.

4. When you finish carving the shape, sculpt in a few details. You can attach buttons, beads, or beans to your sculpture. (Wet the bar of soap where you wish to attach something and push the decoration into the wet area.)

5. Stand your sculpture up on the overturned box, if you want. Be sure to give it a title.

What will you name your soap sculpture?

Little Hands Story Corner™

• *What Is Square?* by Rebecca Kai Dotlich
• *Shapes, Shapes, Shapes* by Tana Hoban
• *Early Learning Skill Builders* (and activity book) by Mary Tomczyk

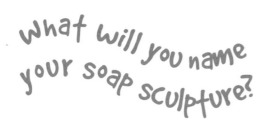

More Little Hands® fun!

▲ **Use it up.** Collect scraps of soap. Wet them and attach them to your sculpture. Or, collect the shavings from soap dishes and put them in a pump bottle with a little water to make hand soap.

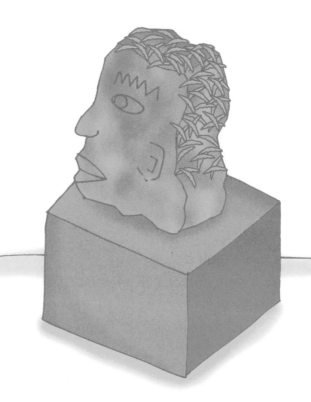

Strip-Paper Sculpture

Little strips of paper,
Made in piles and then stacked.
Cut them, fold them, glue them
on the front and on the back.

Here's what you need:

Newspaper
Child-safety scissors
Colored paper
White glue
Pencil
Styrofoam tray (from fruits or vegetables
    only) or disposable aluminum pie
    plate, for a base

Here's what you do:

1. Cover your work surface with newspaper. Cut
long, thin strips of colored paper. Glue some of
the strips together to make even longer strips.

2. Accordion-fold (see page 23) some of the strips. Roll some strips around a pencil to make curls. Bend some into letters or shapes.

3. Glue some strips on the base in any arrangement you like. Or, hold them above the base and let them fall. Glue them where they land.

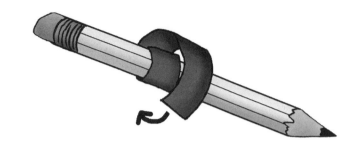

Does your paper sculpture move and sway, or does it stand still?

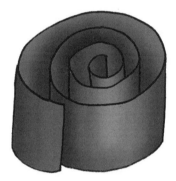

Helping Hands

✳ Many children have a difficult time letting things fall haphazardly. This is a good activity to encourage the freedom to create an unplanned image or shape. For those who insist, let them arrange their pieces as they choose.

More Little Hands® Fun!

▲ **More sculpture fun!** Glue things to your sculpture like dry pasta, glitter, or scraps of material. Use all white paper strips against a dark-colored piece of cardboard. Instead of gluing your sculpture to cardboard, hang it from a string to make a mobile. Use pieces of fluorescent paper to add interest.

string things

String is very movable,
It can twist, curl, and mold.
Make something that's small and curved,
or one that's big and bold.

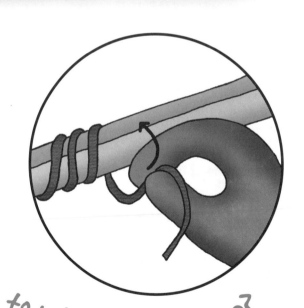

Here's what you need:

Newspaper
String, cut into pieces
White glue mixed with water (1 part glue to
    1 part water) in a shallow bowl or plastic lid
Waxed paper
Tempera paint and paintbrush

Here's what you do:

1. Cover your work surface with newspaper. Soak pieces of
   string in the glue. Transfer the wet string to the waxed paper.

2. Make shapes with the string. (To make a spiral, twist wet
   string pieces around a rolled-up piece of waxed paper.)

3. Allow your shapes to dry.

4. Paint your string shapes.

What causes your string to hold its silly shape?

More Little Hands® fun!

▲ **Make a mobile.** Tie thread to your string things and then hang them from a small branch or clothes hanger. Tie at different lengths so your mobile will have added interest when it twirls in the breeze.

Helping Hands

✳ This activity is another good opportunity to discuss improvising (see HELPING HANDS, PULL-STRING ART, page 8). Put out some crepe paper or tissue paper, colored string, and construction paper. Ask children how they would color their string things if there were no paint handy. What could they use instead of string?

Little Hands Story Corner™

• *When a Line Bends ... A Shape Begins* by Rhonda Gowler Greene
• *Square Triangle Round Skinny* by Vladimir Radunsky

Straw Sculptures

Straws are used for drinking,
But you can use them, too,
For making super sculptures
Just see what you can do!

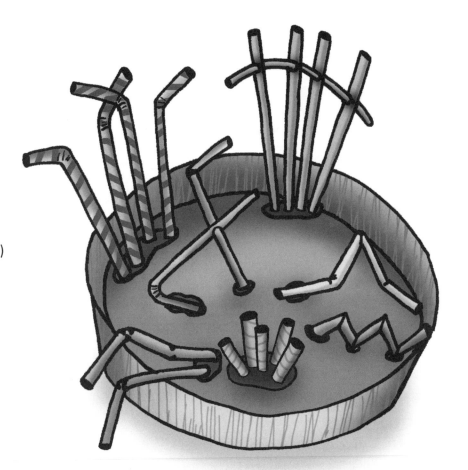

Here's what you need:

Newspaper

Chunk of modeling clay

Styrofoam tray (from fruits or vegetables only)
   or disposable aluminum pie plate

Drinking straws (all kinds and colors)

Hole punch

Child-safety scissors

Here's what you do:

1. Cover your work surface with newspaper.
   Place the clay on the tray or pie plate.

2. Create your sculpture by sticking the
   straws into the clay base.

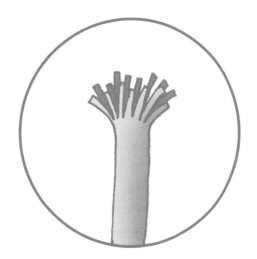
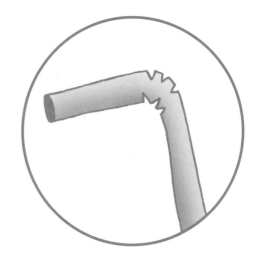

3. Now experiment! Try hole-punching a straw and sliding another straw into the hole. Try trimming a straw on one end to look like an exploding firecracker. Try cutting partway through a straw with little snips to make it bend. Or, use bendable straws along with straight ones.

Do you still think straws are just for drinking?

More Little Hands® fun!

▲ **Straw science.**

• Fill a tall glass with water.

• Insert a straw and then put your finger over the end of the straw.

• Take the straw out of the water while continuing to hold your finger over the end. Hold the straw over a paper towel or empty glass. Release your finger.

• What do you think held the water in and what let it out? (Clue: They are invisible.) If you guessed *air pressure* held the water in and *gravity* let it out, you are right!

✶ Critter Crafts ✶

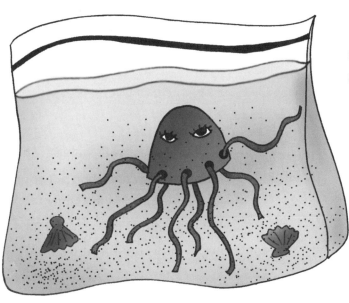

No doubt about it — children love animals. They have a natural fascination with all types of creatures from bugs to turtles, and from those that swim to those that fly. Children sense something almost magical about animals and delight in their diversity. Capitalize on this natural affinity by promoting creative fun while encouraging the development of strong observational skills. Ask children to not only use their imaginations when creating animal art, but to also talk about what they see and hear when they're around animals. Then, set out a wide array of odds and ends along with the usual basic art supplies, and let those little hands create curious critters of their own.

Flitting Butterfly

Nibble on a candy treat,
Save the wrapper from the sweet.
Make a flitting butterfly —
Its shiny wings reflect the sky.

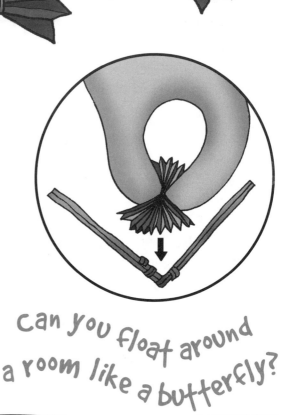

Here's what you need:

Candies, individually wrapped with
cellophane and shiny wrappers
Bag ties, with wire running through them
String, or thread (optional)

Here's what you do:

1. Eat the piece of candy and save the wrappers.

2. Join the twist ties at the ends to make a V shape.

3. Accordion-fold (see page 23) the candy wrapper. Ask for help
if you need it, or instead, simply continue on to step 4, and
then "fluff up" the wrapper "wings."

4. Put the folded wrapper at the bottom of the V shape.

5. Twist the twist ties together above the wrapper. Spread out
the "wings."

6. Curl the ends of the ties to make antennae.

Can you float around
a room like a butterfly?

More Little Hands® fun!

▲ **Butterfly art.** Put several wrappers together so that the wings are different on the top and bottom of the butterfly. ▲ Make a mobile by hanging several colorful butterflies from a stick or edges of a paper plate. ▲ Make a card by gluing a butterfly to a colorful piece of folded paper. Write a special message inside.

▲ **Feed a monarch!** The milkweed plant is the monarch butterfly's favorite food. With a grown-up, transplant some milkweed to a butterfly-safe area like a butterfly garden by your school or a large planter on your patio or steps. Now watch for hungry monarchs to visit!

Helping Hands

✳ Hatching a butterfly indoors is an exciting way to introduce children to the process of metamorphosis, as they observe the caterpillar spinning a *chrysalis,* entering the *pupa* stage, and eventually emerging as a butterfly that they can release (see *Monarch Magic!,* LITTLE HANDS STORY CORNER™). Encourage children to talk about their observations and to share their excitement about the process.

Little Hands Story Corner™

• *Monarch Magic! Butterfly Activities & Nature Discoveries* by Lynn M. Rosenblatt (The life cycle and migration of the monarch butterfly along with learning activities and fun art and crafts. Beautiful photographs, too.)

terrific turtles

Turtles, turtles, we love turtles!
They crawl from place to place.
Some are big and some are small
Let's protect their living space!

Here's what you need:

4-cup section from an egg carton
Hole punch
5 twist ties
Snap lid like the type on a ketchup or shampoo bottle
Permanent markers

Here's what you do:

1. To make the turtle shell, place the egg-carton section with the openings facing down. Ask a grown-up to help you punch holes with the hole punch where the legs and head will be.

2. Thread twist ties through the leg holes and twist to secure.

3. Thread the remaining twist tie through the snap lid and attach it through the head hole.

4. Use markers to draw eyes and a nose on the snap lid.

Pretend you are a turtle out for a stroll!

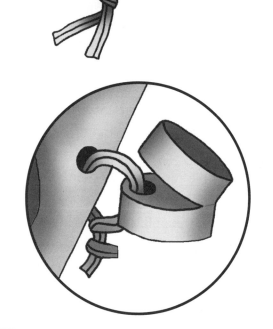

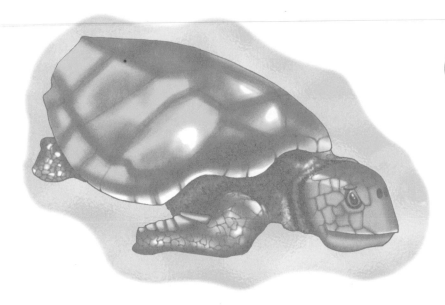

More Little Hands® fun!

▲ **Less and more.** Turtles come in all sizes and weights. Some weigh only as much as two cookies — a lot *less* than babies weigh. Other turtles weigh *more* than you do! Can you name something else that weighs *less* than you do? Can you name some things that weigh *more* than you do?

▲ **Home, sweet home.** Some turtles live in woodsy areas, some live in sandy areas near the ocean's edge, and some live in muddy areas near lakes and rivers. Using a shoebox, construction paper, and tissue-paper scraps, construct a turtle-friendly *habitat* for your turtle.

Helping Hands

✳ Turtles are favorites of almost everyone. They lend themselves to all sorts of interesting early-learning study: compare and contrast; observation; exploration by touching or by guessing and then finding out; and practice with shapes and colors. Plus, children can have simple science experiences that apply those skills to learning about climate, habitat, camouflage, and survival skills. And don't forget the pure excitement and fascination with a creature that carries its home on its back.

Little Hands Story Corner™

- *Little Turtle and the Song of the Sea* by Sheridan Cain
- *The Foolish Tortoise* by Richard Buckley

Stuffed Paper Animals

Make it big or make it small,
It's really up to you.
You decide its shape and color,
Whatever you choose will do.

Here's what you need:

Newspaper
2 sheets of construction paper
Stapler
Pencil
Child-safety scissors
Hole punch (optional)
Yarn, ribbon, or string (optional)

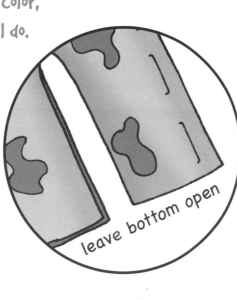

leave bottom open

Here's what you do:

1. Cover your work surface with some newspaper; set aside the rest.

2. Stack the sheets of construction paper and staple them together near the middle. Draw a large animal shape on one piece of paper.

3. Cut out the shape, making sure to cut through both pieces of paper at the same time.

4. Staple the two animal shapes together around the top and sides. Leave the bottom open.

What sound does your animal make?

5. Stuff the animal with crumpled newspaper. Staple the opening shut.

6. Hole-punch around the edges and "sew" yarn, ribbon, or string in and out of the holes, if you like. Ask a grown-up to help you tie the ends together.

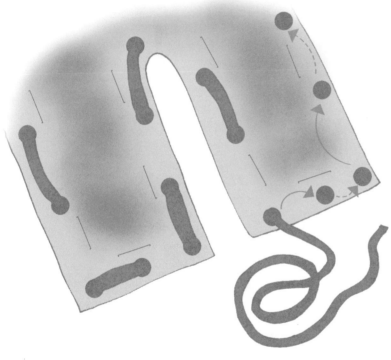

Little
Hands
Story
Corner™

• *At the Zoo! Explore the Animal World with Craft Fun!* by Judy Press. Wonderful, easy crafts and lots to do and learn!

More Little Hands® Fun!

▲ **Make a zoo mobile.** Make more critters. How about a bear, a tiger, or a fish? Paint them different colors and add some glitter, if you like. Use different lengths of yarn to hang them from a stick or clothes hanger.

▲ **Water or land?** Where do your animals live? Are they on land, in the water, or a little of both?

Helping Hands

✳ Here's an opportunity to help a child practice some basic art skills. You may choose to provide some animal-shape *templates,* such as for a fish, a large and a small four-legged animal, and a generic bird. Then, show the child how to *trace* around the template, using it as a pattern. This project also provides the opportunity to *follow the lines* and to *cut with child-safety scissors.*

Cotton-Ball Critters

A furry little caterpillar
May just crawl your way.
or, perhaps a little springtime chick
Is what you'll make today.

Here's what you need:

Newspaper
White glue
Cotton balls
Child-safety scissors
Hole-punch dots and construction-paper scraps

Here's what you do:

1. Cover your work surface with newspaper.

2. Decide what kind of funny, fuzzy critter you would like to make. It can be something real, like a spider, or something pretend.

3. Glue cotton balls together to make the head and body. Cut the cotton balls if you need smaller pieces.

4. Use the dots and cut-out pieces of construction paper to make eyes, a nose, a mouth, a beak, wings, antennae, and claws or paws. Glue them on the cotton-ball body.

What is your cotton-ball critter's name?

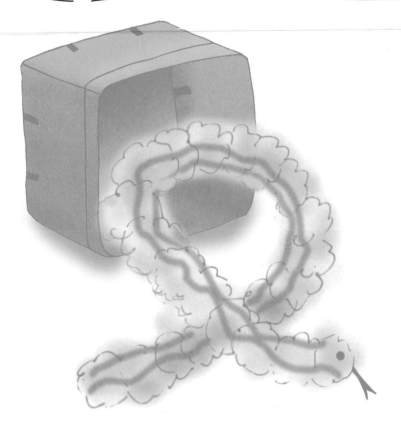

• *I Love Animals* by Flora McDonnell
• *Hey! Get Off Our Train* by John Burningham

Helping Hands

* Set out small piles of cotton balls and other supplies, so children can create several different animals. Younger children might just glue two cotton balls together, but older ones may want to make something quite elaborate.

* Have large bunny templates (see HELPING HANDS, STUFFED PAPER ANIMALS, page 60) ready to use. Children can either glue on a single cotton-ball tail, or they can cover the whole bunny with cotton balls. Have glitter and colored cotton balls available, too.

More Little Hands® fun!

▲ **More art fun!** Use a marker to color white cotton balls. Make a strawberry-basket house for your critter to live in.

▲ **Imagine that!** Tell what your critter's name is, where it lives, what it eats, and whether it is friendly or not.

Snap-Lid Spiders

These friendly little spiders
Can crawl and use a spinner*
To make a super special web
That helps them catch their dinner!

Here's what you need:

Newspaper
Child-safety scissors
Yarn or string
White glue mixed with water (1 part glue to
    1 part water) in a shallow bowl or plastic lid
Waxed paper (optional)
Snap lid, like the type on a ketchup or
    shampoo bottle
Permanent markers
8 buttons or stickers (optional)

Here's what you do:

1. Cover your work surface with newspaper.

2. Cut four pieces of string. Go directly to step 3, or, to
    make stiff legs, soak the yarn or string in the glue.
    Place them on a piece of waxed paper and shape
    as you like; let dry.

Does your spider weave its
web outdoors or indoors?

*A spider's spinner is called a spinneret.

3. Open the snap lid. Place the strings so they are centered across the open lid.

4. Close the lid tight. (Use glue if the lid won't stay closed.)

5. Decorate the lid top with markers. Glue on buttons or use stickers to make "feet" at the ends of the string pieces, if you like.

More Little Hands® fun!

▲ **Capture a spider web.** Did you know you can preserve a delicate spider's web on a piece of stiff paper? With a grown-up's help, gently spray an outdoor web with non-aerosol hair spray or black spray paint (be sure to choose a web that no longer has a spider in it, of course!). Hold the paper behind the web. Pinch off the strands that secure the web so that the web rests on the paper (the wet hair spray or paint will hold it in place). To make the web really stand out against the background, sprinkle it with talcum powder before you spray it.

Helping Hands

✳ Spiders are wonderful critters to introduce to children at a young age. Encourage kids to share their spider stories and to discuss their fears. Then tell some of the interesting things about spiders, such as how they spin their webs, that they have eight legs and wear their skeletons on the outsides of their bodies, and how they are related to the crabs that swim in the ocean!

✳ Take the kids on a friendly spider hunt, where they can observe spiders in windows, along basement walls, and spinning away along fence posts and from tree branches.

Pinecone Reindeer

Nibble on a bunch of grapes,
And save the stems, my dear.
They'll make the special antlers
for your own pinecone reindeer.

Here's what you need:

Newspaper
2 small bunches of grapes
White glue in a shallow bowl or plastic lid
Pinecone
Cotton swab
Small buttons, cotton balls, yarn scraps

Here's what you do:

1. Cover your work surface with newspaper.

2. Eat the grapes. Save the stems.

3. Dip the stem ends into the glue. Insert them into the top of the pinecone so that they look like antlers. Dab on extra glue to hold them in place.

4. Glue on a nose, eyes, and a mouth, using the buttons, cotton balls, or yarn scraps (or whatever is handy).

5. Dip the cotton swab in the glue and dab it on the reindeer. Sprinkle glitter on the reindeer.

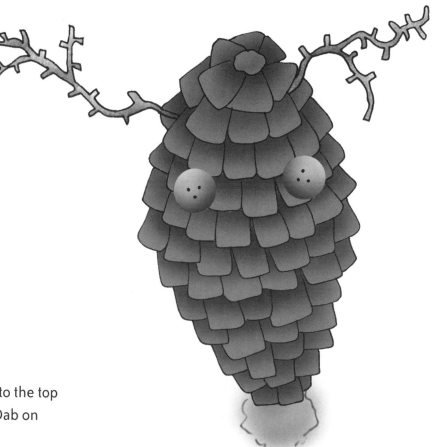

Oh, what a fun pinecone critter you have made!

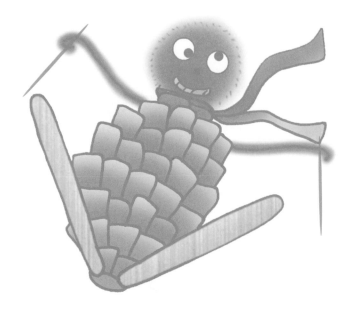

More Little Hands® fun!

▲ **Make pinecone pals.** You can make more pinecone critters by using pinecones of different sizes and different shapes (some are almost round and some are long and thin). You can glue some together, too.

To make pinecone people, here's what you do:

1. Cover your work surface with newspaper.

2. Stand a pinecone on end.

3. Glue a cotton-ball or pom-pom "head" on the top.

4. To make arms, wrap a pipe cleaner or twist tie around the middle of the cone.

5. Decorate your pinecone pal to be anything you want. For example, glue it onto two craft sticks for skis. Put toothpicks in its hands for ski poles.

Helping Hands

✳ Pinecones of all shapes and sizes lend themselves to multiple activities, from learning about nature during a hike to collect pinecones from the forest and using the pinecone "leaves" for mosaics featuring nature's finds, to creating little terrariums or shoe-box habitats for a child's pinecone critters.

Little Sea Creatures

Under the sea there are creatures,
of sizes great and small.
So many diving, swimming critters
We cannot count them all!

Here's what you need:

Newspaper
Large pit from fruit (peach or avocado), washed and dried
Permanent markers or tempera paint and paintbrush (optional)
Child-safety scissors
Tissue paper
White glue
Hole punch
Scraps of construction paper

Here's what you do:

1. Cover your work surface with newspaper.

2. The pit will be the sea creature's body. Paint it or decorate it with markers if you like.

3. Cut fins and gills from the tissue paper. Glue them on the body.

4. Punch some dots out of construction paper. Glue them on to make eyes or to speckle the body.

Would you like to swim all day like a fish?

▲ **How many?** How many things can you name that live in the ocean? Did you name seaweed? An angelfish? A hermit crab?

▲ **Make an "under the sea" diorama.** Create an ocean scene in a shoebox. Use sandpaper for the ocean floor and paint the walls blue. Add small stones and glitter to the ocean floor. Glue tissue-paper sea grass to the walls. Place your sea creatures as if they were swimming in the ocean.

✳ Show children a globe or a map of the world. Count and name the oceans, so that children begin to see the vastness of the world's oceans in relation to the landmasses.

• *Little Hands® Sea Life Art & Activities* by Judy Press
• *Awesome Ocean Science!* by Cindy A. Littlefield

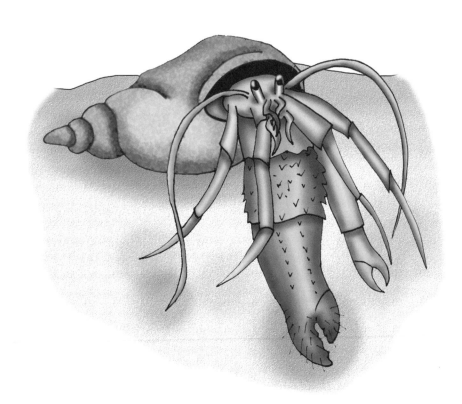

Hermit Crab

Octopus in a "Baggy" Aquarium

Splish and splash the water;
This octopus won't care.
He'll wiggle and he'll jiggle
For he's not going anywhere.

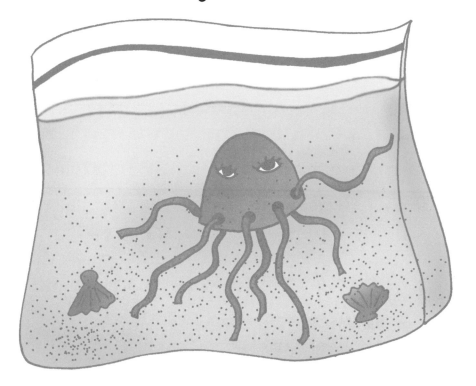

Here's what you need:

Newspaper
Cup from a Styrofoam egg carton
Hole punch
Child-safety scissors
Yarn or heavy cord
Permanent marker
Zip-locking plastic sandwich bag
Water
Glitter (optional)

Here's what you do:

1. Cover your work surface with newspaper. Ask a grown-up to help you punch eight holes around the edge of the egg-carton cup.

2. Cut eight pieces of yarn or cord for long octopus legs. Tie a piece to each of the holes so the legs hang down.

3. Draw eyes on the cup.

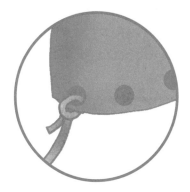

4. Place the octopus in the plastic bag and fill it halfway with water. Shake some glitter into the water, if you like. Tightly close the bag.

5. Gently shake the bag and watch the octopus swim!

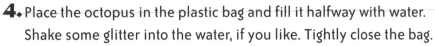

Does your octopus play and sway in the water?

More Little Hands® fun!

▲ **Shell sort.** Gather some shells (use various shapes and colors of dried beans, if no shells are available) and sort them by size, smallest to largest. Then sort them by color, lightest to darkest.

▲ **What would you do?** What would *you* do if you had eight arms like an octopus? Would you eat eight ice-cream cones all at one time? Would you bring all the groceries into the house at once? Would you give lots of hugs?

Little Hands Story Corner™

• *An Octopus Is Amazing* by Patricia Lauber

◢ Slippery Snakes

Instead of throwing socks away,
Think of critters fun to make.
A worm? A slug? Perhaps a snail?
or, a long and slippery snake!

◢ Here's what you need:
Newspaper
Tube sock or leg cut off a pair of pantyhose
Yarn or string
Child-safety scissors
White glue
Felt scraps
Buttons
Needle and thread (optional)

◢ Here's what you do:

1. Cover your work surface with some of the newspaper.

2. Crush more newspaper into balls and stuff the sock or pantyhose leg, filling it as much as you need to depending on what you want to make.

3. Tie off sections of the stuffed sock with pieces of yarn or string, if you wish, or just tie the leg closed at the end. Leave the critter long and thin, or roll it up.

4. Glue felt scraps or buttons on to make a mouth, nose, and eyes. Or, ask a grown-up to help you sew on the buttons, if you like.

Say this three times! "Susie's slippery snake slithers by the sea."

Little Hands Story Corner™

- *Baby Rattlesnake,* told by Te Ata, adapted by Lynn Moroney
- *An Earthworm's Life* by John Himmelman

More Little Hands® fun!

▲ **Make some paper rocks.** All kinds of creatures like to live beneath rocks or sun themselves on the top of warm rocks. Would you like to help them? Here's how!

1. Cover your work surface with newspaper. Cut a brown shopping bag into large flat pieces. Soak them in water.

2. Pour off the water. Using a paintbrush, spatter (see below) watercolor paints all over the pieces.

3. Squeeze the wet paper pieces into tight balls. Set aside to dry.

4. Open the balls. They will be full of cracks and crevices — just like real rocks!

5. Fold the unpainted side back and under.

▲ **How to spatter-paint.** Put some paint on an old clean toothbrush. Point the brush toward the paper. Use a craft stick or side of a pencil to pull the bristles toward yourself. As the brushes snap back, the paint will splash forward.

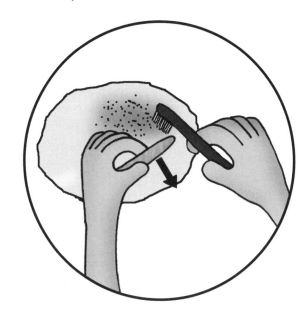

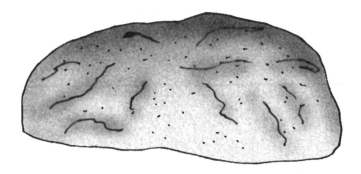

Shredded-Paper Bird's Nest

What is in your bird's nest?
Could it be some eggs?
Or, maybe it's a little chick
With skinny little legs?

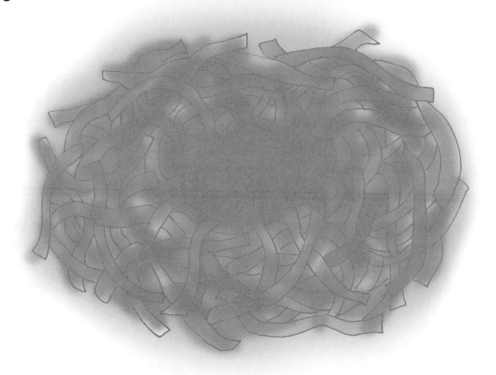

Here's what you need:

Newspaper
Waxed paper
Handful of torn paper, newsprint
   (Sunday's comic section is colorful)
White glue
Child-safety scissors (optional)
Tempera paint and paintbrush (optional)

Here's what you do:

1. Cover your work surface with newspaper.
   Spread out a piece of waxed paper.

2. Mash and twist the shredded paper into a tight clump. Push your fingers down into the center to form a cup.

3. Working on the waxed paper, drizzle glue all over the "cup." (If you squeeze the paper tightly enough, you may not need to hold it together with glue.) Let it dry.

4. Trim off the flyaway pieces, if you wish.

5. Drizzle paint over the nest, if you like. When it's dry, make some cotton-ball chicks (see COTTON-BALL CRITTERS, page 61) to place in the nest.

What do you think will live in your nest?

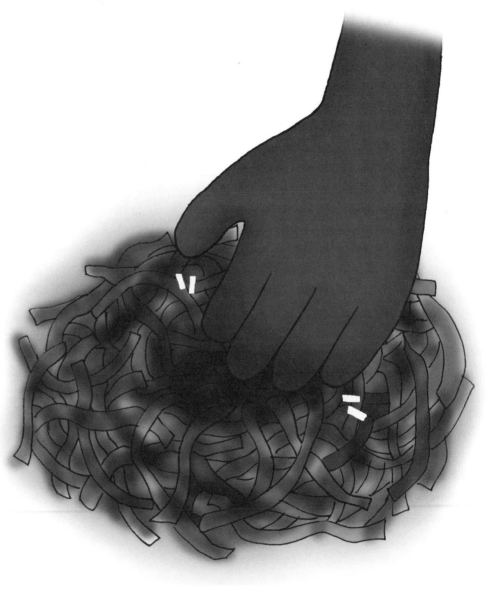

More Little Hands® Fun!

▲ **Help the birds.** Did you know that you can help the birds make their nests in the spring? All you need to do is find some pieces of yarn or string, scraps of fabric, or some lint from the dryer and leave it outdoors in the bushes. The birds will find it and use it in their nests. You'll be helping them build their homes with pretty colors, too!

Helping Hands

✳ Of course, not only familiar birds like robins make nests. Introduce children to all kinds of nests: raccoon nests up in the trees, huge osprey nests on poles, squirrel nests, and even little mice nests. The best times to hunt for nests on a nature walk are in the fall when they have been abandoned and in the early spring before the trees have fully leafed out.

Pencil-Shaving Sheep

Don't toss old pencil shavings;
Please save them in a heap.
Create a little baby lamb,
or some silly woolly sheep!

Here's what you need:
Newspaper
Pencil
Paper, any color or weight
Paintbrush
White glue mixed with water
  (1 part glue to 1 part water)
  in a shallow bowl or plastic lid
Pencil shavings in a plastic sandwich bag

Here's what you do:
1. Cover your work surface with newspaper.

2. Draw a sheep or a lamb. Make it big to fill the paper.

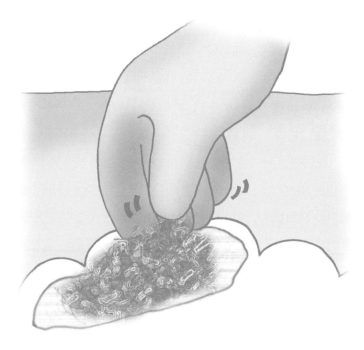

3. With the paintbrush, apply the glue-water mixture to a small area of your drawing. Sprinkle the pencil shavings over the glued area. Repeat the gluing and sprinkling process until the sheep are nice and "woolly."

4. Press down very lightly to be sure the shavings stick to the paper. Turn the picture over and gently shake off the excess onto the newspaper.

Baa! Your sheep sure are woolly, aren't they?

More Little Hands® fun!

▲ **Special art effects.** Isn't it fun to see what special art effects, like your sheep's "wool," you can make with odds and ends around your house or classroom? What else might you use to make a special art effect? What about using uncooked elbow macaroni to make hair or dried beans and peas for a nature picture?

▲ **Save shavings from colored pencils.** Then, use them on your picture. Or, color the shavings by adding powdered paint to the sandwich bag and shaking it.

▲ **More critters!** Use your pencil shavings to make animals with fur. Then, cut them out and place them on a picture or mural of a farm or woodland.

• *Is Your Mama a Llama?* by Deborah Guarino
• *Good Night, Gorilla* by Peggy Rathmann

✷ Creating Usable Art ✷

⊺o the adults: Children change the form and function of an object by using their imaginations. A child will unwrap a present from a large box, remove the gift, and after playing with it for a short time, turn her attention to the empty box, which presents all sorts of creative play opportunities. The box may become a spaceship, a house, a pirate's ship, or a time capsule.

Help children develop their natural creativity by supplying them with odds and ends that they can turn into very different things. You can present the projects as shown here, but always allow the child to do his own thing with the suggested materials. Most of all, have fun with your child or children while making usable art!

Marvelous Mesh Hat

A hat like this is unique
And really fun to wear.
So decorate it as you wish,
Then set it atop your hair.

Here's what you need:

Mesh bag like the ones oranges,
 onions, or potatoes come in
Child-safety scissors
Ruler
Decorations: ribbon, buttons,
 beads, stickers, yarn, etc.

Here's what you do:

1. Ask a grown-up to help you cut off the top of
 the bag, about 10" (25 cm) above the bottom.

2. Fold over or roll down the edge of the bag
 several times. (If there is a paper label running across the center of the bag, leave it on
 and fold down that section.)

Cut here

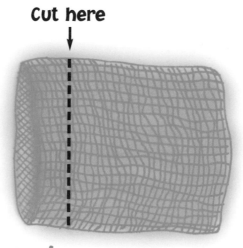

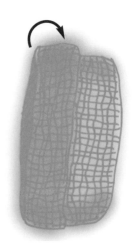

wow! Your hat is so cool!

3. Tie ribbon and/or yarn to the holes. Hang buttons, beads, and stickers on the yarn. Or, weave ribbon in and out of the holes in the bag.

▲ **Make party hats!** At your next birthday party, have each of your friends make a hat. How about adding some crepe paper streamers hanging down the backs of the hats so they wave as you swing your head?

Helping Hands

✳ Let children suggest other things that can be used as hats, such as a paper plate or a scarf. Talk about how hats often let us know what a person's job is, using examples like a chef's hat, a police officer's hat, a clown hat, and a hard hat. Encourage children to think about which professions have special headgear and why.

Little Hands Story Corner™

• *Zoe's Hats* by Sharon Lane Holm

Carry-All Caddy

Make a special caddy,
And you'll find sure enough
That you have lots of uses
For a thing to hold your stuff.

☑ Here's what you need:

Newspaper

Empty four- or six-pack cardboard drink
   carton with a handle

Sticky-backed paper

Child-safety scissors

Permanent markers

Stickers

Plastic bottles or jars, cut down to fit into
   the carton sections (optional)

☑ Here's what you do:

1. Cover your work surface with newspaper. Have a
grown-up help you cover the sides of the carton
with pieces of sticky-backed paper.

2. Decorate the sticky-backed paper with markers
and stickers. Put your name on it if you want.

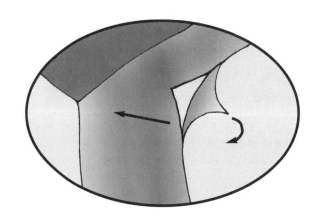

3. Slip the bottles or jars into the carton sections, if using.

4. Fill each section with favorite art supplies, toys, or things you like to collect to carry around with you.

What will you put in your carryall?

▲ **Comfy handle.** Wrap yarn or tape around the handle to make it easier to hold.

▲ **Use as a "critter carrier."** The carton's sections are perfect for holding little stuffed animals. You can play that you are taking them to the veterinarian for a check-up or bringing them outdoors for a picnic.

Helping Hands

✳ This activity provides children with a chance to categorize items. Sorting is an important early-learning skill that involves comparing and contrasting objects for size, purpose, etc. All pens can go into one section, all paintbrushes in another, etc. Or, a child can sort toys in different ways — from smallest to largest, for example.

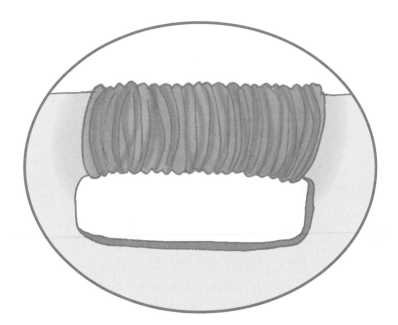

Twisted-Paper Jewelry

Will you make a present
for a friend who's on your list?
What fun you'll have creating
This jewelry that you twist.

◢ Here's what you need:

Newspaper
Child-safety scissors
Construction paper in various colors
Ruler
Water in a sink or shallow pan
Paper towel
White glue
Spring-type clothespins
Decorations: ribbon or yarn, stickers, markers

◢ Here's what you do:

1. Cover your work area with newspaper.

2. Ask a grown-up to show you how to use child-safety scissors to cut the construction paper into strips. For a bracelet, cut a strip about 6" x 12" (15 cm x 30 cm). For a ring, cut one about 2" x 4" (5 cm x 10 cm). For a necklace, cut three strips about 6" x 12" (15 cm x 30 cm).

3. Soak the strips in the water. Shake off the excess. Blot with a paper towel.

4. For a bracelet or ring, roll the strip into a long, thin band.

Carefully twist the band.

Tuck one end into the other and glue. Hold together with a clothespin until dry.

5. For a necklace, roll and then twist all three pieces. Tuck the ends together to make one long piece; glue to secure.

Tuck one end into the other and glue. Hold together with a clothespin until dry.

6. When the jewelry is thoroughly dry, decorate it. (See MORE *LITTLE HANDS* FUN! on page 85 for some good ideas.)

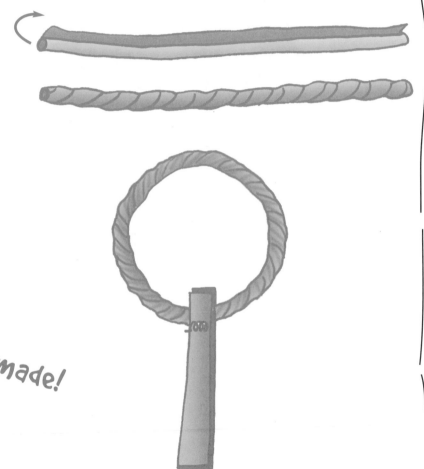

What pretty jewelry you've made!

Little Hands Story Corner™

- *What's Next, Nina?* by Sue Kassirer
- *I Feel Orange Today* by Patricia Godwin

More Little Hands® fun!

▲ **Make it shine!** Glue on glitter.

▲ **Design a matching set.** Be a jewelry designer who makes matching sets of jewelry, all decorated in a similar way. Try gluing on beads and buttons.

▲ **Jewelry wraps.** Wrap different colors of tape around the jewelry to make it jazzier (and stronger). Or, wrap it in tin foil to give it a silvery look! Glue stickers and beads on your foil wrap.

Helping Hands

✳ This activity is a perfect opportunity to suggest giving gifts as a sign of caring for friends. Encourage little ones to make a present of jewelry to show how they feel about a friend or loved one.

Wacky Hat

This hat is snazzy-jazzy,
Not quiet, meek, or mild.
So add a lot of zany things
And make your hat real wild!

Here's what you need:

Newspaper
Clean bottom of a gallon (3.7 L) plastic jug
    or large, heavy-duty paper plate
Permanent markers
White glue
Decorations: buttons, stickers, paper scraps,
    pom-poms, etc.
Hole punch (optional)
Ribbon or yarn (optional)

Here's what you do:

1. Cover your work area with newspaper.

2. Draw on the jug's bottom or the paper plate with
the markers. Glue or stick on other decorations.

What is the silliest hat you've ever seen?

3. Ask a grown-up to help you punch holes around the edges, if you want. Hang ribbon or yarn from the holes. Or, weave ribbon or yarn in and out of them.

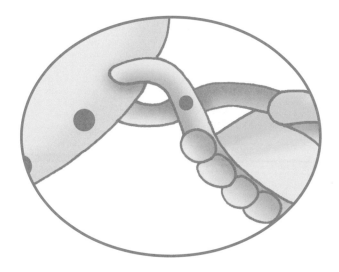

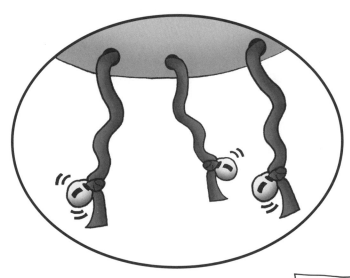

Helping Hands

✳ If you want to simplify this activity, use a large, heavy-duty paper plate instead of the jug. Then follow directions, being sure to use ribbons for tying under chins.

✳ This is a wonderful opportunity for self-expression. Ask the children why they decorated the hats as they did. How do they feel when wearing the hats?

More Little Hands® fun!

▲ **Dramatic play.** How do you feel when you are wearing your hat? Act out what you would do if you were wearing the hat you made. Would you be a fancy lady? A firefighter? A construction worker? An artist?

▲ **Tie it on.** To keep your hat on securely, tie ribbons to the holes on both sides. Then tie a bow under your chin.

▲ **A musical hat.** Glue on bells or dangle them from ribbons. Now you'll make music when you walk!

tube Hideaway

What will you hide, down inside
Your little carryall?
Mini cars? Tiny candy bars?
or a super bouncing ball?

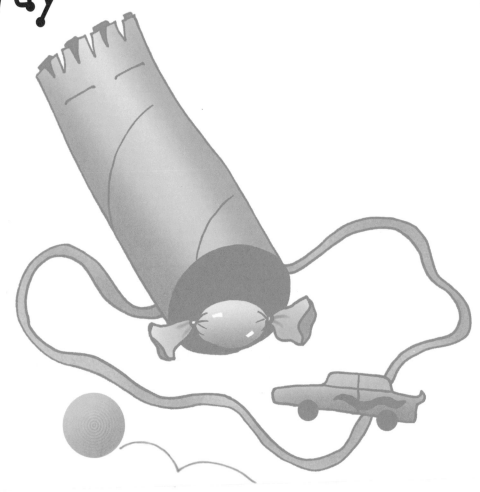

◢ Here's what you need:

Newspaper
Cardboard tissue or paper towel tube
Stapler
Hole punch
String or yarn

◢ Here's what you do:

1. Cover your work surface with newspaper.

2. Fold the tube flat. Staple one end closed.

3. On the opposite end, have a grown-up help you punch one hole in the center of each side. Use the creases as guides.

4. Lace the ends of the string or yarn through the holes so you can hang the tube or wear it around your wrist or neck.

Peek-a-boo! What's hiding inside your hideaway?

▲ **Play "Guess what's inside?"** Give the others a hint as to what is inside your carryall. Each person gets two guesses (fewer than three players = each gets three guesses). If someone guesses correctly, they get to go next. If not, show everyone what's inside, and you pick who goes next.

▲ **Spatter-paint your hideaway.** Put some paint in a shallow lid. Dip the bristles of an old, clean toothbrush in the paint. Hold the brush toward the tube. Pull a craft stick over the bristles toward yourself. The paint will spatter forward away from you and onto the tube.

▲ **Make a carryall with a lid.** Have a grown-up help you cut the top of a large tube to a make a flap. Fold the flap over the opening and tuck it inside for a lid.

Helping Hands

✳ Children who are more adept with scissors may want to fringe the end of the tube on the stapled end.

✳ This is a good sharing activity when one child makes a hideaway for another child. Children may want to exchange hideaways filled with little gifts or candies.

Denim-Pocket Plaque

What do you do with old jeans?
Turn them into fun!
Cut them, glue them, fill them up
With anything under the sun.

◢ Here's what you need:

Newspaper
Square of fabric with a pocket in the
    center cut from a pair of old jeans
White glue
Piece of cardboard or poster board, a
    little larger than the fabric square
Hole punch
Yarn

◢ Here's what you do:

1. Cover your work area with newspaper.
Glue the pocket piece to the cardboard
or poster board.

2. Have a grown-up help you punch holes
at the top outside edges of the cardboard or poster board.

3. Tie a piece of yarn to the holes to make a hanging plaque.

4. Put whatever you'd like into the pocket. Hang your plaque.

This recycling is fun — and handy!

Helping Hands

✳ *Sorting* and *categorizing* are important early-learning skills. They help children begin to organize a group of items into subgroups, a skill they will need forever after. Also, sorting involves *observational skills, compare and contrast skills, color recognition,* and, in some cases, good *tactile skills,* such as when you sort rough stones and smooth stones.

More Little Hands® Fun!

▲ **Play "big, bigger, biggest."** Make a long plaque with several pockets in a row. With a partner, sort items by size into the pockets.

▲ **Decorate your pocket plaque.** Glue on beads, buttons, ribbons, glitter, dry pasta, feathers, sequins, and pom-poms to the pocket and the backing.

Newspaper Mat

You can make a "sit-upon"
That's white and black and flat.
Weave the paper in and out
To make a paper mat.

Here's what you need:

12 unfolded newspaper sections,
about 22" x 25" (55 cm x 62.5 cm)
Stapler
Tape

Here's what you do:

1. Working on the floor is easiest, because the mat will be quite large. Starting at the bottom, fold an opened newspaper section in half three times to make a long piece. Repeat to make 11 more pieces.

2. Staple both ends of the pieces.

FOLD

3. Lay out six pieces, long sides touching. Tape the edges to a table or the floor to hold them in place while you work.

4. Carefully weave one of the remaining pieces over and under the taped-down pieces. Allow each piece to stick out slightly at each end.

5. Repeat with the next piece, except this time go *under,* then *over.*

More Little Hands® Fun!

▲ **Make a "funny" mat.** Use the comics section to make a more colorful sit-upon. Or, make a patchwork mat by coloring the different squares with markers. Then, write your name by putting each letter in a separate square.

▲ **What's new?** In the newspaper, you can find out what teams won their games, what movies are playing in the theater, what is happening around the world, and what the weather forecast is where you live. Do you ever look at the newspaper at home? Do you like to look at the photographs?

6. Continue weaving with the remaining pieces, one over and under, and the next one under and over.

7. Fold all edges over or under and tape them in place. (See HELPING HANDS.)

Helping Hands

✳ Edges that are tucked in are neater (step 7), but this is difficult for small children to do. Taping them is easier.

✳ Point out different sections and features of the newspaper like the "comics," "headlines," "bylines," and "captions." This is a good opportunity to begin a home or classroom newspaper. Every week, let each member of the household or some of the students contribute to the newspaper. They can each write an article with their byline, headline, and a caption if photos or art work are available.

Your mat is perfect for sitting on while you listen to a story!

✷ Make-and-Play Art! ✷

To the adults: Play is such a wonderful learning experience for children. They learn to get along with others or amuse themselves; they learn to follow instructions or use their imaginations; they learn new skills or perfect those they've tried before; they learn about feelings, about their five senses, about team work, and about compromise. Best of all, playtime is a time to giggle, exercise, and think without boundaries.

Art is a creative extension of this play process where children are free to create, build, and explore as they grow socially and emotionally. And what could be better than encouraging children to make the things that they play with! It is a perfect opportunity for them to discover how creative energy is expressed in so many ways.

Cork Town

People, animals, and birds —
Who knows what this town brings?
Everything is made of cork
And lots of extra things.

Here's what you need:

Newspaper
Fine-tipped markers
Corks from bottles
White glue
Round toothpicks
Decorations: scraps of paper, string, fabric,
    yarn, glitter, cotton balls, etc.

Here's what you do:

1. Cover your work surface with newspaper.

2. With the markers, draw faces on the corks.

3. Glue on clothing, cotton-ball "hair," or whatever you
    like to decorate the people or animals. Stick toothpicks
    in the corks to make arms and legs.

Can you make a cork doggie? How about a person fishing?

More Little Hands® fun!

▲ **Create a village.** Make milk-carton houses for the cork people.

▲ **All aboard!** Make EGG-CARTON BOATS (see page 38) and take the cork people for a boat ride.

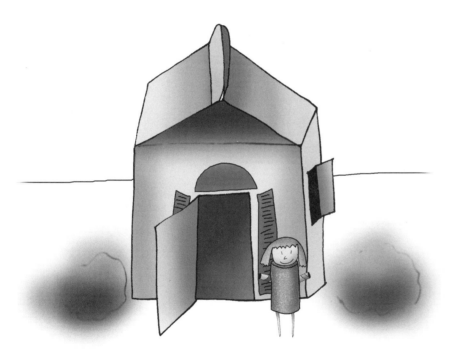

Helping Hands

✳ The story of cork is a great topic for conversation that tests children's imaginations. Open the topic up by asking kids how many things they can think of that are made from cork. Then ask them where they think it comes from. That can lead into a fun discussion of the cork trees growing in Portugal on cork farms and how it is harvested (it is the bark removed from trees) only every nine years.

✳ Many "throwaway" items can be reused as fun objects for little hands at play. This not only inspires creativity, it encourages recycling efforts as well. Provide children with objects to examine and let them suggest artistic uses based on the shape or material.

Magnet-Motor Mover

Will you make a car or critter?

Will it move fast or slow?

You're the magnet-motor mover,

Deciding how fast, and where, to go!

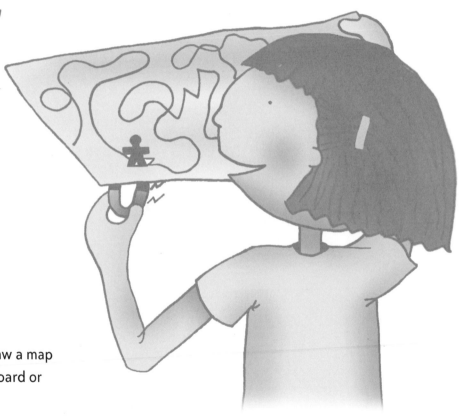

Here's what you need:

Newspaper

Markers or crayons

Piece of white cardboard or poster board

White paper

Child-safety scissors

White glue or tape

Paper clip

Magnet (not bendable kind or small
   refrigerator magnets)

Here's what you do:

1. Cover your work surface with newspaper. Draw a map
   of roads and a town on one side of the cardboard or
   poster board.

2. On the paper, draw a little person, critter, or car that
   you want to have traveling on the map.

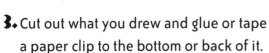

3. Cut out what you drew and glue or tape a paper clip to the bottom or back of it.

4. Hold the magnet on the back of your map. Place the paper clip on top of the map opposite the magnet.

5. Use the magnet to make your creation move across your map!

Magnets sure are fun!

More Little Hands® fun!

▲ **Flip it!** Turn the magnet over. What does the paper clip do?

▲ **Take a magnetic walk.** Go around the room with the magnet to see what other things are attracted to it. What things are *not* attracted to it?

▲ **On your mark, get set, go!** Make several paper-clip creations and have a race with some friends.

Pocket Pop-Up Pal!

Make a hiding pop-up pal
That waits deep in your pocket.
It jumps up high and says "Hello"
When you do unlock it!

◢ Here's what you need:

Newspaper
Child-safety scissors
Colored paper
Fine-tipped markers
White glue in a shallow bowl and a cotton swab, or tape
Empty plastic dental-floss container with the insides
    removed, or a small box with lid that fits inside
    your pocket

Note: Please read HELPING HANDS on page 102
before you begin this activity with children.

◢ Here's what you do:

1. Cover your work surface with newspaper.

2. Cut a long, thin strip of paper slightly narrower than
    the bottom of the dental-floss container or box.

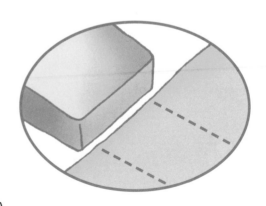

3. Draw a face on one end of the strip. Glue or tape another small piece of paper under the head to make arms.

4. Accordion-fold (see page 23) the first strip so that it will tuck down inside the container or box.

5. Using a cotton swab, dab a little glue in the bottom of the container or box, being careful not to get it on the sides. (If this is too difficult, tape the bottom of the strip into the bottom of the container.) Press the bottom of the strip into the glue.

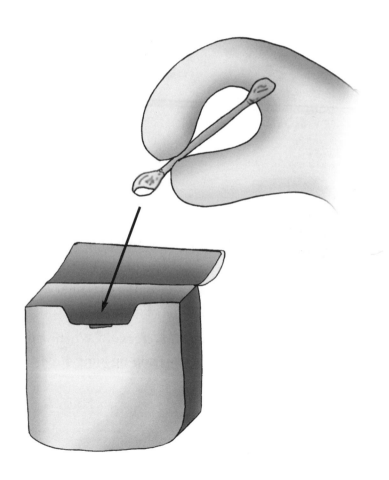

6. After the glue is dry, fold the rest of the accordion into the container or box.

7. Close the lid. Make your pop-up jump out whenever you wish.

Will you hide your pop-up in your pocket?

More Little Hands® Fun!

▲ **Make a silly monster!** Add plastic "wiggly" eyes or yarn hair to your pop-up. How about antennae? Tape a paper strip to the outside of the container and put your monster's name on it.

▲ **Sing "Pop Goes the Weasel."** When you sing, "pop," make your pop-up jump out like a jack-in-the-box.

Helping Hands

✳ If a child finds working with a small dental tape box and a narrow strip of paper too difficult or frustrating, by all means make a POCKET POP-UP PAL that resembles a jack-in-the-box, rather than this small pocket version. It can be made the same way, only on a larger scale using a larger box and a wider and longer strip of paper. Little ones will be very pleased with it.

✳ Older children will, however, love playing with their pocket pals, as little pocket toys are a great favorite. They are a little secretive, which makes each child feel special, and also quite comforting during trying moments. Plus, accordion-folding such a narrow strip of paper and fitting it inside the small container will help develop coordination and fine motor skills.

Peanut Puppets

These itsy-bitsy puppets
Are fun and really neat!
While you collect the shells,
You have the nuts to eat!

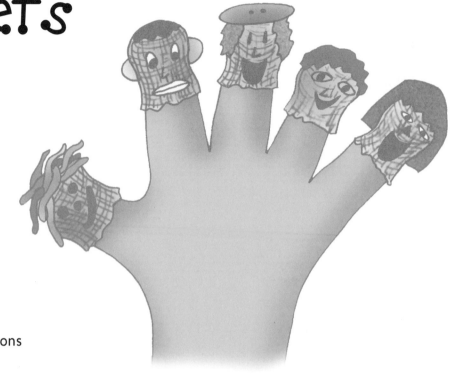

Here's what you need:

Newspaper
Peanuts in the shells
Fine-tipped markers
White glue
Child-safety scissors
Decorations: cotton balls, yarn, glitter, and buttons

Here's what you do:

1. Cover your work surface with newspaper. Carefully break open the peanut shells so that each half remains in one piece and will fit on the tips of your little fingers.

2. Use the markers to make eyes, noses, and mouths on the peanut shells to create people, animals, monsters, or whatever you like.

3. Glue cotton balls or yarn pieces to the shells to make hair or fur. How about a button for a hat?

4. Now, slip the peanut shells on your fingers and have a mini puppet show.

Oh, your puppets are so much fun! Great job!

More Little Hands® fun!

▲ **Glue ribbon "arms"** to your peanut person so you can shake and dangle them.

Helping Hands

✳ Let the children examine the outside of the peanut shell and feel its texture. Suggest they hold it close to their ears and shake it. Can they hear how it rattles around in the shell without breaking? Ask if they've ever eaten "boiled peanuts." How do the texture and the flavor change?

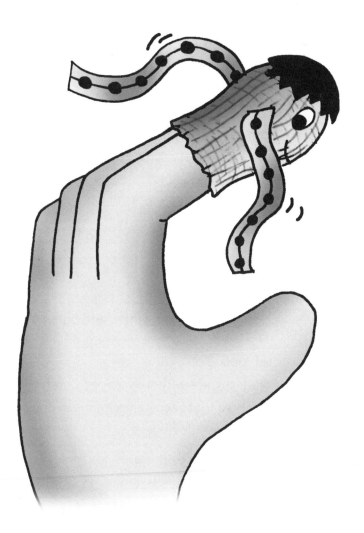

Paper Pom-Poms

Such neat strips of paper
A shredder sure can make!
But we know it's better
for making pom-poms to shake.

▨ Here's what you need:

Newspaper
Plenty of thin paper strips cut from recycled paper,
    or from a paper shredder
Stapler
Tape
Craft stick or drinking straw (optional)

▨ Here's what you do:

1. Cover your work surface with newspaper. Put about 20 strips of paper together at one end and secure with a staple. Use a variety of colors, if possible.

2. Make four or five stacks of 20 strips, and secure them together with tape.

3. Add the craft stick or straw for a "handle," if desired.

It's time for a parade!

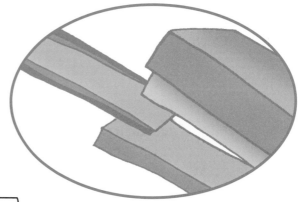

▲ **March around.** Isn't it fun to march? Ask an adult to put on some marching music such as John Philip Souza's, and then march around the room or the outdoors, raise your pom-poms high, and keep time with the music.

▲ **Tambourine fun.** Need an easy way to keep the beat with your pom-poms? Make a tambourine! All you need are two aluminum pie plates, some dried peas, tape, and ribbon. Place the dried peas in one pie plate. Then, cover it with the other pie plate, inverted. Tape the edges together. Add ribbons to flutter as you tap your tambourine over your head. What fun!

Helping Hands

✳ Marching is so much fun and the pom-poms make it special. Have children practice standing tall, lifting their heads high, and walking to the beat of the music. If they want, have them make some costumes, too.

Mixed-Up Picture Fun

A person's head on a doggie?
Your own face on a cat?
With crazy, mixed-up pictures
You might create just that!

◤ Here's what you need:

Newspaper
Child-safety scissors
Old magazines
Old photographs of family and friends
Paper (optional)
White glue (optional)

◤ Here's what you do:

1. Cover your work surface with newspaper. Cut out some pictures of people and animals from the old magazines.

2. Cut out some people and animals from the old or duplicate photographs.

3. Cut the heads off the bodies. Now make funny combinations by mixing and matching the heads and bodies.

4. Glue them onto paper if you like.

You can make some very funny pictures!

More Little Hands® fun!

▲ **Name your creatures.** Tell about its "traits." Would your brother's head on a dog's body make him hungry for doggie biscuits?

▲ **Make a puppet.** Glue your creature to a craft stick. Now act out a story using your crazy character. Try changing your voice so your puppet talks in a silly voice to match the silly way it looks.

▲ **Make a storyboard.** Glue lots of different faces and bodies onto a big piece of paper. Tell what's happening in the scene you created.

Helping Hands

✳ While the skill level to *make* these pictures is a 2, the skill level to *play* with them is a 1.

✳ A fun and easy way to make these to use repeatedly is to glue them to felt, and then trim the felt around the pictures. Now make the cuts of the heads from the bodies, and if the picture is big enough, from the legs, too. Make a felt board by covering a piece of poster board with a contrasting felt piece. Now you have something kids can enjoy in the future as well as immediately!

Tap, Tap, Tap Dancer

Tap! Tap! Tap! What a great sound!
You can make it with your feet.
Dancing high, dancing low —
create a rhythm and a beat!

Here's what you need:

Newspaper
Child-safety scissors
Cardboard tissue or paper towel tube
4 strips of paper, 5" x 12" (2 cm x 30 cm)
White glue or staples
2 paper clips
Yarn or string

Here's what you do:

1. Cover your work surface with newspaper. Ask a grown-up to help you cut a ½" (1.5 cm) circle off the end of the cardboard tube for a head.

2. Fold one of the long strips in half for the body.

3. Loop it through the "head" and fold the body down. Glue or staple in place.

4. Accordion-fold (see page 23) the other three strips.

5. Slide one strip between the folds of the "body." Glue or staple in place for arms.

6. Glue or staple the ends of the other two strips to the bottom of the body for legs. Slip paper clips onto the ends of the legs for tap shoes.

7. Tie a piece of yarn or string from the head. Make your marionette dance!

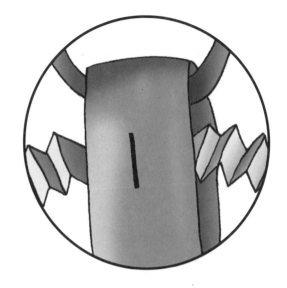

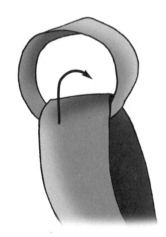

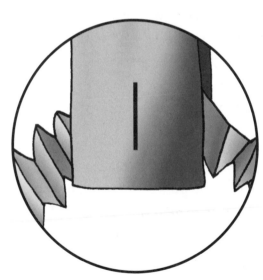

Can you tap dance along with your TAP, TAP, TAP DANCER?

More Little Hands® fun!

▲ **Jazz up your dancer.** Decorate a cupcake liner or coffee filter for a skirt and glue it in place. How about yarn hair?

▲ **Tap shoes make a great sound.** Try dancing your tap dancer on various surfaces. Listen to the different sounds the paper clip "tap shoes" make.

Helping Hands

✳ Dancing is a fun way to practice coordination and to develop large motor skills while developing music appreciation. If possible, rent a film with Gene Kelly tap dancing, such as *Singin' in the Rain*. Encourage the children to tap out the rhythms with their hands or their feet. Then, invite them to get up on their feet and move to the music — tapping or not.

catch 'ems

It's fun to try to catch things
With a toy that you create.
Count up your score. How did you do?
Wow! That is great!

Here's what you need:

Newspaper

Permanent markers

Clean, dry half-gallon (2 L) plastic jug
    with handle and cap, with the bottom
    cut off (or, for older children, a plastic
    soda bottle with the bottom cut off)

Fine-tipped markers

Piece of yarn, about 24" long (60 cm)

Large button or cork

Tape (optional)

Here's what you do:

1. Cover your work surface with newspaper.
   Decorate the outside of the container as
   you wish.

2. Remove the cap of the jug or bottle. Put the end of the yarn down into the neck of the container. Screw the cap back on to hold the yarn in place.

3. Tie the button or cork to the other end of the string. Secure with tape if necessary.

4. Hold the container upside down by the handle. Swing it and try catching the button or cork in the upturned container.

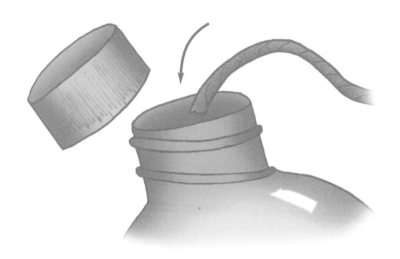

How many catches did you try to make?

● **More Little Hands® fun!**

▲ **Catching advice.** Learning to catch is not an easy thing to do, so if you are having trouble, don't worry about it. Here's one thing you can try: Keep your eye on the ball or cork or whatever you are trying for. Don't look at your hand — just the object. It really helps. Good luck!

Helping Hands

✳ Heavier objects are easier to catch in the CATCH 'EM. Plastic buttons work well. Encourage kids and if they become too frustrated, switch to rolling a ball and then try bouncing it low so kids can catch it in their CATCH 'EM.

Special Day Crown

Trim this crown with things you'd like
To wear on a special day.
Birds and flowers, balls and bats —
Whatever you like to play!

✂ Here's what you need:

Newspaper
Construction paper, assorted colors
Ruler or tape measure
Pencil
Child-safety scissors
White glue
Markers
Stapler
Decorations: glitter, buttons, crepe paper, or
    curling ribbon

✂ Here's what you do:

1. Cover your work surface with newspaper. Select a
    piece of colorful paper.

2. To make the crown, measure and mark the paper, so it will be
    about 9" (22 cm) wide and long enough to fit around your head. Cut
    pointed triangles or zigzags along one long side of the paper strip.

3. Depending on the day you are celebrating, draw and cut out objects that you want to put on your crown. For someone's birthday, consider decorating the crown with different-colored paper candles or pictures of the person's favorite things to do.

4. While the crown is still flat, glue on the decorations you made. Add different trims such as glitter, streamers made with ribbon or crepe paper, or wildflowers. Let the glue dry.

5. Write a name or a special day on the crown with markers, if you wish. Ask a helper to help you wrap the crown around your head (or the birthday person's head) and staple the ends together, making sure the smooth part of the staple is on the inside.

Hurrah! Today is a special day!

More Little Hands® fun!

▲ **Make any day special!**
Birthdays are always lots of fun and very special, of course, but you can celebrate other special days, too. How would you decorate your crown to celebrate Arbor Day, when people plant and care for trees? What about a Valentine's Day crown, or one for Mother's Day? And what would you put on your crown to celebrate today? How about a Friendship Crown with smiling faces, or people shaking hands?

Helping Hands

✳ This activity is a great way to focus positive attention on someone who needs to feel special on any given day, while helping others to think about what makes a person special. It is also a good way to introduce the idea of symbols, such as a birthday cake; patriotic colors like red, white, and blue; or red Valentine's Day hearts.

Little Hands Story Corner™

• *Little Hands® Celebrate America!* by Jill Frankel Hauser (learning activities)
• *Kids' Pumpkin Projects* by Deanna F. Cook (autumn fun)

Color-Your-World Viewer

So many things around us —
oh, what can they be?
Look out through this viewer
And explore the world you see!

Here's what you need:

Newspaper

Clean, empty plastic syrup bottle, preferably
   with a handle, with the bottom cut off

Permanent markers

Child-safety scissors

Colored cellophane

Rubber band or tape

Here's what you do:

1. Cover your work surface with newspaper. Decorate the
   container with the markers.

2. Look through the viewer and describe what you see.

3. Cut a piece of cellophane. Hold it in place over the bottom
   of the bottle with the rubber band or tape.

4. Now look through the viewer. How do things look now?

More Little Hands® fun!

▲ **Draw what you see.** With markers or crayons, draw the view through the cellophane.

▲ **Hold the container at different angles.** How does the view change when the container is closer or farther away from an object?

▲ **Experiment.** Look through other kinds of bottles and different colors of cellophane. Does one work better than another?

Does the cellophane change what you see?

✳ Activity Listing by Skill Level ✷

 Level 1 activities

Color-Your-World Viewer, 116–117

Cotton-Ball Critters, 61–62

Dryer-Lint Sculpture, 36–37

Food-Color Fuzzies, 20–21

Grapevine Tree, 40–41

Hole-Punch Magic, 10–11

Marvelous Mesh Hat, 79–80

Masking-Tape Surprise, 18–19

Paper Pom-Poms, 105–106

Peanut Puppets, 103–104

Popcorn People, 14–15

Potato "Snow" Scene, 26–27

Pull-String Art, 8–9

Shredded-Paper Bird's Nest, 73–75

Slippery Snakes, 71–72

Stamping Sponge Fun, 31–32

Tissue Twists & Shapes, 44–45

Tube Hideaway, 88–89

Wacky Hat, 86–87

 Level 2 activities

Carry-All Caddy, 81–82

Catch 'ems, 112–113

Coffee-Filter Flowers, 22–25

Cork Town, 96–97

Denim-Pocket Plaque, 90–91

Egg-Carton Boat, 38–39

Flitting Butterfly, 55–56

Little Sea Creatures, 67–68

Magnet-Motor Mover, 98–99

Mixed-Up Picture Fun, 107–108

Octopus in a "Baggy" Aquarium, 69–70

Pinecone Reindeer, 65–66

Pretend Milk Glass, 34–35

Robot Fun!, 42–43

Snap-Lid Spiders, 63–64

Special Day Crown, 114–115

Straw Sculptures, 52–53

String Things, 50–51

Terrific Turtles, 57–58

 Level 3 activities

Foil Relief Art, 16–17

Grocery Mesh-Bag Stitchery, 12–13

Moovey-Groovy Art, 28–30

Newspaper Mat, 92–94

Pencil-Shaving Sheep, 76–77

Pocket Pop-Up Pal!, 100–102

Soap Sculpture, 46–47

Strip-Paper Sculpture, 48–49

Stuffed Paper Animals, 59–60

Tap, Tap, Tap Dancer, 109–111

Twisted-Paper Jewelry, 83–85

Index

A

accordion folds, how to make, 23

E

early learning skills, 58
    color recognition, 21, 24, 32
    counting, 68
    letter recognition, 19
    shape recognition, 9, 10–11, 16–17
    sorting/categorizing, 21, 70, 82, 91
    tracing shapes, 60
    using senses, 28–30

G

games, 37, 89, 91, 99, 112–113
gift-giving, activities for, 9, 35, 85, 89

H

hats, 79–80, 86–87, 114–115

I

improvising, 9, 51

L

Little Hands Story Corner™, 13, 27, 30, 32, 39, 47, 51, 56, 58, 60, 62, 68, 70, 72, 77, 80, 84, 115

M

materials, activities using
    cardboard tube, 88-89, 109–111
    cotton balls, 61–62, 65–66,
    egg carton, 38–39, 57–58, 69–70
    foil, 16–17
    newspaper, 73–75, 92–94
    straws, 22–23, 52–53
    string/yarn, 8–9; 12–13, 50–51, 63–64, 69–70, 71–72
    Styrofoam trays/aluminum pie plates, 36–37, 40–41, 48–49, 52–53
musical/rhythmic activities, 87, 102, 106, 109–111

☉

outdoor/nature activities
    birds' nests, 75
    ocean habitat, 68
    pinecones, collecting, 66

planting
    milkweed for monarchs, 56
    seeds, 25
    spiders, 64
    tree activities, 41
    turtles' habitats, 58

P

puppets, 108, 109–111

R

recycled materials, using creatively, 5, 7, 33, 78, 97

S

safety tips, 6
science concepts
    air pressure, 53
    gravity, 53
    metamorphosis, 56
sewing activities, 12–13, 59–60
spatter painting, 45, 72, 89

T

templates, using, 60, 62

More Good Books from Williamson Publishing

If you enjoyed using *Little Hands® Create!*, you may be interested in our other books for this same age group. *Little Hands®* books for children ages 2 to 7 (and the adults in their lives) are 120 to 160 pages, fully illustrated, trade paper, 10 x 8, $12.95 US/$19.95 CAN. To order, please see the last page.

Little Hands®
CELEBRATE AMERICA!
Learning about the U.S.A. Through Crafts & Activities
by Jill Frankel Hauser

Little Hands®
SEA LIFE ART & ACTIVITIES
Creative Learning Experiences for 3- to 7-Year-Olds
by Judy Press

Parents' Choice Recommended
Little Hands®
EARLY LEARNING SKILL-BUILDERS
Colors, Shapes, Numbers & Letters
by Mary Tomczyk

Parents' Choice Gold Award
FUN WITH MY 5 SENSES
Activities to Build Learning Readiness
by Sarah A. Williamson

ForeWord Magazine Bronze Award
ALL AROUND TOWN
Exploring Your Community Through Craft Fun
by Judy Press

Parents' Choice Recommended
AT THE ZOO!
Explore the Animal World with Craft Fun
by Judy Press

Parents' Choice Recommended
EASY ART FUN!
Do-It-Yourself Crafts for Beginning Readers
by Jill Frankel Hauser

Parent's Guide Children's Media Award
ALPHABET ART
With A to Z Animal Art & Fingerplays
by Judy Press

American Institute of Physics Science Writing Award
Early Childhood News Directors' Choice Award
SCIENCE PLAY!
Beginning Discoveries for 2- to 6-Year-Olds
by Jill Frankel Hauser

WOW! I'M READING!
Fun Activities to Make Reading Happen
by Jill Frankel Hauser

Parents' Guide Classic Award
Real Life Award
The Little Hands ART BOOK
Exploring Arts & Crafts with 2- to 6-Year-Olds
by Judy Press

Parents' Choice Approved
The Little Hands BIG FUN CRAFT BOOK
Creative Fun for 2- to 6-Year-Olds
by Judy Press

Parents' Choice Approved
Little Hands FINGERPLAYS & ACTION SONGS
Seasonal Rhymes & Creative Play for 2- to 6-Year-Olds
by Emily Stetson and Vicky Congdon

AROUND-THE-WORLD ART & ACTIVITIES
Visiting the 7 Continents Through Craft Fun
by Judy Press

Parents' Choice Approved
Little Hands PAPER PLATE CRAFTS
Creative Art Fun for 3- to 7-Year-Olds
by Laura Check

ARTSTARTS for Little Hands!
Fun Discoveries for 3- to 7-Year-Olds
by Judy Press

The Little Hands PLAYTIME! BOOK
50 Activities to Encourage Cooperation & Sharing
by Regina Curtis

American Bookseller Pick of the Lists
RAINY DAY PLAY!
Explore, Create, Discover, Pretend
by Nancy Fusco Castaldo

Parents' Choice Approved
The Little Hands NATURE BOOK
Earth, Sky, Critters & More
by Nancy Fusco Castaldo

MATH PLAY!
80 Ways to Count & Learn
by Diane McGowan and Mark Schrooten

Visit our Website!

To see what's new at Williamson and to learn more about specific books, visit our website at:
www.williamsonbooks.com

To order Books:

Toll-free phone orders with credit cards:
1-800-586-2572

We accept Visa and MasterCard *(please include the number and expiration date).*

Or, send a check with your order to:
Williamson Books
535 Metroplex Drive, Suite 250
Nashville,TN 37211

For a free catalog: **mail, phone, or fax (888-815-2759)**

Please add **$4.00** for postage for one book plus **$1.00** for each additional book.
Satisfaction is guaranteed or full refund without questions or quibbles.